Vengeance

VENGEANCE

The Fight Against Injustice

PIETRO MARONGIU
and
GRAEME NEWMAN

ROWMAN & LITTLEFIELD
Publishers

ROWMAN & LITTLEFIELD

Published in the United States of America in 1987
by Rowman & Littlefield, Publishers
(a division of Littlefield, Adams & Company)
81 Adams Drive, Totowa, New Jersey 07512

The frontispiece shows Clytemnestra killing Cassandra,
whom Agamemnon had brought back from the Trojan
War. *Museo de Spina, Ferrara.*

Library of Congress Cataloging-in-Publication Data

Marongiu, Pietro, 1946–
  Vengeance : the fight against injustice.

  Includes index.
    1. Revenge. 2. Revenge—Social aspects.
I. Newman, Graeme, R. II. Title.
BF637.R48M37   1987   302   86-29647
ISBN 0-8476-7540-8

89 88 87
6 5 4 3 2 1

Printed in the United States of America

The righteous shall rejoice when he seeth
the vengeance: he shall wash his feet
in the blood of the wicked.
So that a man shall say, Verily there
is a reward for the righteous.
—Psalms 58: 10, 11.

Contents

Foreword, Ernest van den Haag   ix

Acknowledgments   xi

Introduction   1

1 The Elementary Sense of Injustice   9

2 Vengeance as Anger   24

3 From Vengeance to Justice   36

4 Vengeance and the Sacred: Dante's Inferno   48

5 Vengeance and Responsibility: Hamlet's Procrastination   60

6 Cultures of Vengeance   69

7 The Political Economy of Vengeance   90

8 Vengeance as Protest: Jesse James and the Bandit Legend   103

9 Brokers of Vengeance: The Mafia   125

10 The Lone Avengers: An Impossible Mission   146

Conclusion   164

Index   171

Foreword

THE LORD, THROUGH MOSES, commands "Thou shalt not avenge."[1] Further, the Apostle Paul quotes Him, "Vengeance is Mine."[2] Often these passages are interpreted as a repudiation of vengeance as morally wrong. This is incorrect. The Lord clearly reserves vengeance to Himself. The ancient notion of Hell—everlasting punishment—certainly indicates that He means it, that those who unrepentently violate His commands will be punished with relentless severity. The divine wrath lasts forever—there is no parole from hell.

Further, the Apostle Paul does not object to vengeance when carried out on this earth provided it is not done privately but by authority. "The ruler," he writes in the same epistle to the Romans,[3] is "a revenger [meant to] execute wrath on him that doeth evil."

Despite biblical support, vengeance has acquired a bad reputation in modern times. It is, at best, regarded as a barbaric and irrational relic, disruptive of social life, morally unjustifiable, and repudiated by everyone formally in authority, as well as by those who aspire to moral authority, e.g. clergy. Yet, oddly, revenge lives on, as Graeme Newman and Pietro Marongiu make abundantly clear. Why does it? What social and psychological functions does vengeance have? What transformations did it undergo? Can it be morally justified? How, finally, is vengeance related to other social institutions and functions?

The authors of this thought provoking and engaging book ask these questions within a rich historical and conceptual analysis. Their answers are tentative and often quite frankly

---

1. Lev. 19:18
2. Rom. 12:19
3. Rom. 13:4

ix

speculative. Given the subject, it could not be otherwise. But both the questions and the answers are never less than stimulating.

We owe much gratitude to these diligent scholars who have taken it upon themselves to explore a difficult and unpopular subject and to remind us, that like it or not, disguise it every which way, or admit it candidly, the desire for revenge for any injury, real or fancied, is universal. We will cope with it the better the more we learn about it. *Vengeance: the Fight Against Injustice* can teach us a great deal about a shared and important human disposition, the understanding of which is indispensable if one wishes to understand history and human nature.

ERNEST VAN DEN HAAG

Acknowledgments

WE ARE IN DEBT to more persons than it is possible to mention because they have contributed to the birth and development of the many ideas contained in this book. Each of us, however, wishes to mention some special people who have helped make this book possible.

Pietro Marongiu thanks Giovanna Montgomery who, since the project's beginning, has provided constant support and unswerving confidence, helped him through the most difficult periods, and ensured this volume's successful completion. He would also like to thank Duilio Casula, Rector Magnificus, University of Cagliari.

Graeme Newman thanks his wife Joan, and their children Tamsin, Clancy, and Amanda for putting up with his preoccupation with vengeance, and for being understanding about the time spent writing when other more rewarding activities of family life took second place.

Both authors are especially appreciative of the support of their mutual friend Franco Ferracuti, University of Rome.

The desolate landscape of Sardinia, the School of Criminal Justice of the University of Albany, and downtown Manhattan provided almost ideal environments where most of our work was accomplished.

PIETRO MARONGIU
GRAEME NEWMAN
New York City

Vengeance

Introduction

I have a compact with the dead. But if I could get this man, my soul
would finally be at peace.

> Simon Wiesenthal referring to his
> lifetime search for Mengele, reported
> in *Time Magazine*, September 26, 1977

Do you feel that taking the law into one's own hands, often called
vigilantism, is justified by circumstances?

> —Always: 3%, Sometimes: 68%, Never: 23%
> *Newsweek* poll, March 11, 1985

Thou shalt give life for life, eye for eye, tooth for tooth, hand for hand,
foot for foot, burning for burning, wound for wound, stripe for stripe.

> *Exodus* 21: 23, 24, 25

The Universal Force of Vengeance

VENGEANCE HAS THE POWER of an instinct. The "lust for vengeance," the "thirst for revenge," are so powerful that they
rival all other human needs. Indeed, as we shall see in this
book, people will sacrifice their own lives, undergo tremendous hardship, and devote their entire lives to see that vengeance is done. It is carried out by many different kinds of
people, together and alone, and in many different settings
throughout the world. The vehement and horrifying nature of
the vengeful act is enough to convince us of its instinct-like
power.[1]

Erich Fromm, in his book, *The Anatomy of Human Destructiveness*, defines vengeance as a spontaneous form of aggression; an explosion of destructive impulses that are activated
by special circumstances, usually those perceived as threaten-

1

ing survival. Vengeance, Fromm says, is incredibly destructive because of its "innate" intensity, and its spontaneous reaction to perceived, unjustified suffering inflicted on the individual or group. He argues that this form of aggression is different from "normal defensive aggression" (that is, aggression that seeks to preserve life) for two reasons: 1. The vengeful, aggressive act is performed in cold blood, after the damage has been done, and therefore is not a defense against immediate danger; 2. It is of great intensity, often crude, vicious, and insatiable. Unfortunately, this definition does not precisely fit all cases of vengeance. Furthermore, it suggests that vengeance is not a "normal" reaction, but, at the same time, Fromm recognizes that vengeance is a reaction exhibited all over the world, and is indeed, universal.[2] It is difficult to see how a universal reaction can also be considered abnormal.[3] The Bernhard Goetz case illustrates this paradox.

Mr. Goetz had been mugged while travelling on a New York subway, as a result, he obtained a handgun. About two years later, when confronted by four black youths who demanded money from him in a subway car, he shot all four of them. Interpretations of the actual facts vary considerably. Some suggest that he acted in self defense, others that it was a vigilante style shooting:

> Bernhard Goetz, celebrated "subway vigilante" describes his reactions as those of "rage," "like a cornered rat." "I was out of control," he said on the "20/20" NBC program. When one of four black youths had demanded $5, Goetz shot all four, two of them in the back; the fourth a second time.[4]

Goetz's actions can be interpreted as aggression, both in anticipation of violence, but also as a result of past damage, since Goetz had, two years previously, been mugged. In this case, it would seem to be utterly impossible to distinguish between self-protection and vengeance. Goetz's actions seemed to have been aimed at both preserving his own life and destroying the lives of his aggressors. In one sense, one could say that he prepared himself (bought a gun and carried it with him) for the time when he would be threatened by subway thugs. But it is also apparent that his reaction in the actual situation was that of "spontaneous rage," most likely precipitated by the instinct-like force of vengeance. Goetz subsequently made statements that clearly reflect a vengeful frame of mind, such as the following in relation to the mugger who had injured his kneecap: "[He] should be given the option of obtaining an early release if he lets someone take a baseball bat and take his best shot at cracking his knee."[5] Nor does Fromm recognize that vengeance may be cold-blooded, and in this sense very rational.[6] An act of vengeance can be a passionate, violent reaction, but it can also be carefully and systematically calculated. The following case clearly shows this "cool-headedness" and can hardly be called "spontaneous" in the sense that it was uncontrolled or impulsive. But there is no doubt that the motive *was* vengeance, and the fact that it was so controlled suggests that this reaction exists in our culture as a valued way of dealing with a perceived injustice:

> At the trial of Steven Todd Jenkins, the deputy District Attorney of Minnesota, Thomas Fable, testified that Jenkins was an expert marksman who had long planned the ambush of the bankers who had forclosed on his father's farm. Jenkins was sentenced to life imprisonment.[7]

The Confusion of Vengeance with Crime

In his book, *Punishing Criminals*, Ernest Van den Haag defines vengeance as an individual or collective reaction aimed at the satisfaction of the desire for retaliation by the injured party.[8] Here, its private character is recognized. The initiator of the action is the individual or group that has been wronged, not an external source of authority commissioned to administer justice by inflicting punishment. The vengeful act is begun arbitrarily by whichever party feels offended, and does not seem to be defined by pre-existing rules in proportion to the immediate "offense."

In this regard, we must note that the juridical norms that have, throughout history, come to define and redefine crimes, did not occur in the primeval period of vengeance with respect to the shared rules of the group. That is, the primitive origin of juridical norms is private, not collective.[9] This is why early definitions of "wrongs" were extremely ambiguous and lacking in consensus—arbitrary and defined according to the sense of injustice felt by the injured party. We see this clearly among those who reap revenge in order to cancel out an offense, yet these same persons are perpetrating the very same behavior (or worse) that they wish to avenge:

> Robert Lee Moody's father sexually molested his sisters, forced his mother into prostitution, and split open his elder brother's head with a screw driver causing irreparable brian damage. After becoming a born again Christian, Robert sighted his father down the barrel of a 12-gauge shotgun and literally blew him apart. It was a slaying in cold blood, but public opinion approved: last week state Judge Eric Younger sentenced Robert to two years' missionary service.[10]

Viewed outside the context of a "social order," the ambiguity of these acts of vengeance is unmistakable—it is impossible to distinguish between the crime and the punishment.[11] How does one separate the two? It can only be done by an appeal to authority.[12] What kind of authority, of course, is another matter. Sometimes the legal authority will pronounce its judgment, but often in the case of vengeful acts, popular opinion is enough to ensure that the law bends to the "people's authority." The following cases are clear examples:

Vengeance as community sentiment: As the *Newsweek* poll at the beginning of this chapter demonstrates, there is strong popular support for vengeance—strong enough to be called a *demand* for vengeance. The case of the town bully who was murdered is a case in point.

> Maryville, Mo. July 22 UPI. A six-member coroner's jury ruled yesterday that the killing of an unpopular Skidmore resident outside a bar on July 10, apparently by a vigilante mob, was the work of 'person or persons unknown.' The decision was reached despite the testimony of Tina McElroy, 24 years old, that she could identify the man that shot her husband once in the head.[13]

Legal tolerance of vengeance: A father was so outraged by the kidnapping of his son that he lay in wait, and murdered the kidnapper. There was an outpouring of public support, and the sentence he eventually received expressed this support.

> A karate instructor accused of kidnapping one of his students died today of a gunshot wound to the head. The student's father, Gary Plauche, ambushed the kidnapper as he was being escorted from Ryan Airport. He was subsequently found guilty of murder, and sentenced to one year's probation, according to the news program, "20/20."[14]

Advocacy of vengeance by community leaders: President Reagan and Mayor Koch were reported to have made approving comments concerning Bernard Goetz's actions. While Mayor Koch did not go as far as the mayor in the case below, he nevertheless recognized the rage that individuals feel when they are victims of violence, having been himself attacked.[15]

> Buffalo, July 29. On the morning of July 5, a 10-year-old girl was abducted and raped, and that night her father was arrested and charged with stabbing the man accused in the case. Since then, the father, Willie Williams has become a celebrity, and has received extensive local support. "I've got two daughters, one 13 and one 11, and if a guy raped my daughter, he would have got the same thing from me," said Mayor James Griffin.[16]

Perhaps "crimes," as they are called today, are but approximations of original offenses perceived at various stages throughout history as a result of particular vengeful actions. Without a third party to define such offenses as "crimes," there exists the typical progression or spiralling process by which each offense is countered by another offense more severe until the complete destruction of one of the parties is achieved. It is the establishment of a social order that attempts to break into this cycle of destruction. This order may take on many forms, but in its early stages, it usually consists of a group of elders who are external to the warring factions. A range of techniques of pacification is adopted, such as the ratification of a marriage between members of the factions, perhaps the first act of public justice! Even when pacification seems to work, latent hostility may remain indefinitely, and may suddenly reappear in response to what may seem on the surface to be a very minor provocation.

It would seem that the only enduring solution to this destructive process is the development of a shared acceptance of a system of social control, which is always present in a developed society. This is the assumption that underlies Mayor Koch's assertion that, while he understands the rage felt by victims of violence, nevertheless one must not use violence in retaliation except within the constraints of the law. We have seen from the above examples that the law can sometimes treat the avenger leniently. However, if the avenger feels that the legal system is inadequate to bring about the "deserved" punishment of the offender, the motivation to act alone becomes very strong:

> Tony Cimo thought justice, sure and swift, would execute the killer of his parents. But the killer appealed his death sentence, and after several years still remained alive behind bars, while Cimo sat up

nights by the gravesides of his parents thinking of the killer still breathing. Finally, Cimo paid one of the killer's fellow prisoners to kill him, and kill him he did. Cimo, now 36 and father of two, was sentenced to eight years for conspiracy to murder. "I don't think you are a hardened ciminal and need to be put away for a long time. But, in order to deter others, I am going to incarcerate you," said the judge.[17]

While the actions of Cimo are hardly those of a hero, his motivations are certainly understandable and applauded by some, other lone avengers are often seen as heroes. The initial media treatment of Bernhard Goetz is an excellent example. However, in this case, and perhaps all those we have described so far, the *morality* of their acts is the subject of hopeless debate because the act of "punishment" is virtually the same as the act being punished. Nor is the morality of this problem solved by having the legal system carry out the punishment if the motivation remains the same—vengeance. When done by a legitimate "authority," vengeance is given the more sanitary term of "retribution," but this makes it no more moral than the private act. It simply makes it legitimate.

In sum, vengeance is a recognized form of social control, and partly because it receives this recognition, controversies continue over whether these acts are "crimes" or "virtues," and whether the actors are heroes or villains. However, it is our view that the question of the morality of vengeance is of secondary importance because we will show that it is actual physical domination that is primarily involved in the act of vengeance. Morality is more commonly invoked as a later rationalization to justify the act. Why morality must be invoked to "excuse" vengeance is examined in the early chapters as we analyze the maturation and growth of vengeance from the "primitive" to the "civilized."

Fromm (1983) suggests that the passion for vengeance is deeply rooted "in the need for security present in all groups." What does he mean by the "need for security?" We interpret this to mean that there is a deep cultural need in Western culture (and probably all major cultures of the world) to see that vengeance is carried out. The questions we seek to answer are: Where does this need come from? Why has it become so intense? What forms has it taken throughout the development of our culture? Our way of answering these perplexing questions is to identify the origins of vengeance in civilization, trace its development, and outline its various forms of growth in Western society. We show how it has become "civilized," and how it has become perverted into practices that seek to justify the excessive use of violence against others. We suggest that vengeance is basically motivated by a concern for equality, justice, and reciprocity, but that the story of civilization is one in which reciprocity is constantly pitted against society's concern and need for the antithesis of reciprocity—the demand for obedience, the maintenance of social order.

The problem that we face today is the same as that faced by our ancestors, the ancient Greeks: how to strike the balance between reciprocity and obedience, how to prevent either of these processes from getting out of hand.

Notes

1. Fromm generally identifies two types of aggression: (1) benign-defensive aggression common in all animal species, phylogenetically programmed, aimed at preserving the species by either attack or flight when vital interests are threatened and (2) malignant, destructive aggression, which appears essentially uncontrolled (that is not phylogenetically programmed), more typical of humans than animal species because humans are less driven by "instincts." Fromm argues that animals, because their aggression is instinctual, have built-in limits to their aggression, so that they rarely fight to the death. Humans, in contrast, have no such built-in limits, thus the tendency to uncontrolled destruction. Erich Fromm, *The Anatomy of Human Destructiveness* (New York: Holt Rinehart & Winston, 1983, pp. 272–76, K. Lorenz in *On Aggression* (New York: Harcourt Brace Jovanovich, 1967) make a similar point.

2. Fromm discusses the diffusion of "blood vengeance" throughout the world, observing that: (1) It is a sacred sentiment observed individually and collectively by members of a clan; (2) it is a process without an end because of its spiralling nature (no crime can be totally expiated without bringing on itself another crime); (3) it has, paradoxically, with the penal codes a "certain utility" to conserve a measure of social stability.

3. The only way one could make such an argument would be to claim that everyone was "abnormal."

4. This and other material relating to the Goetz case has been taken from the extensive coverage this case has received in national and local media, from January through March 1985.

5. *The New York Times*, February 26, 1985.

6. Fromm does recognize, however, that there are many different levels of intensity in vengeance that contrast with the hypothesis of spontaneous aggression. We are, however, concerned here with a difference in *kind* rather than intensity.

7. From *The New York Times*, April through June 1984.

8. E. van den Haag, *Punishing Criminals* (New York: Basic Books, 1975).

9. Here we contradict Durkheim's theory of the origin of punishment.

See E. Durkheim, *The Division of Labor* (New York: The Free Press, 1964), chap. 2.

10. *Newsweek*, March 5, 1984, p. 58.

11. Indeed this paradox has been recognized by Donald Black in his seminal article, "Crime as Social Control," *American Sociological Review* 48 (1983): 34–45.

12. Nils Christie also recognizes this fact in his creative *Limits to Pain* (Oxford: Martin Robertson, 1983).

13. *The New York Times*, July 29, 1981, sec. 12, p. 5.

14. Taken from *The New York Times*, March 19, 1984; and television program *20/20*, March 21, 1985.

15. *20/20*, March 21, 1985.

16. *The New York Times*, August 1, 1983.

17. *Albany Times Union*, June 21, 1983, p. 1.

1

The Elementary Sense of Injustice

It is . . . extremely probable that myths are distorted vestiges of the wishful fantasies of whole nations, the secular dreams of youthful humanity.

—Sigmund Freud[1]

ALL ACTS OF VENGEANCE arise from an elementary sense of injustice, a primitive feeling that one has been arbitrarily sugjected to a tyrannical power against which one is powerless to act. The sense of injustice is essentially a product of the interplay between domination and subordination. Vengeance is a punitive act of coercion motivated by an elementary sense of injustice. We distinguish between two basic models of punishment: the reciprocity model and the obedience model. Vengeance is essentially concerned with reciprocity, but because it originates in the domination and subordination process, it is also inseparable from the quest for obedience. Indeed, because of its coercive nature, vengeance, in its development, is constantly mingled with obedience. This constant interplay between reciprocity and obedience informs us of the many variations of vengeance that have arisen throughout the development of Western society.

We can trace the early development of vengeance in Western society by examining its myths. The dawn of our culture is expressed in different myths, some cruel, depending on the traditions from which they spring. While we confine ourselves to myths of the Western world, it is apparent that many mythical themes seem to be universal, existing as they do, across diverse cultures. For example, Kirk, in his work on the nature of Greek myths, observed that the myth of the castration of Uranus, which we will describe shortly, has strict parallels in the Near East.[2]

These myths were first handed down orally and the vast literature now available supports their common origin. Naturally, there has been a tendency to modify the stories, but they have retained their basic structure remarkably well. This is very significant when one considers that the oral transmission of stories would surely have fostered their transformation and distortion. When one examines the similarities of the basic myths in different cultures with different languages, one would have expected considerably more variation. It is reasonable to surmise, therefore, that the myths express a certain universality of the human condition.

We may regard the literature on the Greek myths as a systematic codification of Greek culture from the period of Homer and Hesiod during the eighth and seventh centuries B.C. to the pinnacle of Greek tragedy[3] during the fifth century B.C. It is not our intention to examine here the different interpretations of the myths (such as the functionalist, psychoanalytic, or that of structural anthropology), though their contributions are of considerable interest. Rather, we are concerned, at this point, with showing that the myth, as a traditional narrative, provides us with a rich source of data concerning the cultural justification and historical use of punishment. It expresses the psychological and political elements of our culture, which are the building blocks of a punitive society.

Although each generation does perhaps make its own changes and adjustments to the myths, nevertheless, the basic structure of the myths remains constant—because basic human needs are constant. This constancy has encouraged students of culture to hypothesize the existence of phenomena such as the "conscience collective" as defined by Jung, whose work drew heavily on myths and legends.[4] But now, it is time for our story. One of the earliest Greek myths tells of the creation of the world.[5]

The Myth of Creation

Earth (Ge) was first of all things. She created the mountains, the valleys, and the desolate fuming sea. The Sky (Uranus) married Ge who gave birth to the Titans (six sons and six daughters), to the Cyclopes (monsters with only one eye), and to three giants who had one hundred hands and fifty heads.[6]

Uranus became so hostile towards his young children, that he held them prisoner in a hole in the ground, never letting them see the light of day. He derived a deep sense of inner happiness from this deed.

Naturally, his wife suffered deeply, so much so, that she began to plot how she could free her children and punish her unjust husband. To this end, she fashioned a huge scythe with large teeth from the iron that was hidden in her womb. She then asked her children to help her carry out her act of vengeance.

The sons were afraid; none had the courage to act decisively because each feared the father's reprisal. Finally, the youngest son—the great Kronos, god of cunning said: "Mother, I made a promise and I will carry it out. I care nothing for my father's odious name. Besides, by his own despicable action, he has already made the choice for me." Ge gave Kronos the scythe and showed him where he could hide until the night, when the sky would come alone to meet the earth, embracing her completely in its arms.

The sky came. With his left hand, Kronos seized his father's genitals, and with a fierce single blow, cut them off and threw them into the sea. A few drops of blood fell to the ground, and from them, the three Furies were born—goddesses who were later to punish parricide and other crimes against kinship. And when the mutilated member of Uranus fell into the sea, masses of white foam bubbled up—and the goddess of love, Aphrodite, was born.

By this violent act, Kronos seized absolute power, and he has retained this powerful image in mythology ever since. He is Time who, carrying his great scythe, proceeds inexorably. He is the master of life and death.

Fresh from his victory over the starry sky, Kronos began to behave in the familiar way of new revolutionaries: he began to get rid of his allies. He exiled his brothers the Cyclopes, the Titans, and the Giants to Tartar (a sinister underground place as far away from earth as it was from the sky). He took as his wife his sister, Rhea, the Titan queen, who gave him three sons and three daughters, one of whom was Zeus, the future king of the gods. According to some, Zeus was the first born to Kronos, but others think he was the youngest, just as his father was the last born of Uranus.

If the reign of Uranus was tyrannical, that of Kronos was no better. In fact, Kronos, convinced by a prophecy that one of his sons would one day overthrow him, was even more terrible than his own father. He ate each of his children as soon as it was born. But Kronos was also foiled by his wife. When she gave birth to Zeus, instead of giving Kronos the new born baby, she gave him a big stone that was wrapped in swaddling clothes. Kronos swallowed it without realizing the substitution. Rhea then hid Zeus on the island of Crete, where he would wait to fulfill his destiny.

Much time passed until Zeus overcame Kronos through sheer force and cunning. He waited for Kronos to become drunk on honey, then when he fell asleep, Zeus mounted a surprise attack, put his father in chains, and forced him to give back the brothers and sisters whom he had swallowed. Zeus then sent Kronos into exile to the Beatitude Islands, where, though confined to the earth, he still reigned. In mythology, this period is remembered as the "golden age."

Zeus also freed the Cyclopes who, in return, gave him the power of thunder and lightning—a clear recognition of his new power. Yet Zeus, uneasy about the will of the gods, wishing to avoid the fluctuating fortunes that they often brought on him, felt impelled to fight the Titans to the end— the same Titans he had liberated. This war lasted for ten years, until finally Mother Earth suggested a winning strategy for Zeus to follow.

He hired the three one hundred-handed Giants (Cottus, Briareus and Gyes) who, with a storm of three hundred stones, subdued the Titans, put them in chains, and sent them back to Tartar. Hesiod says that there arose, when the Titans were finally put down, a night "as black as three nights in one." The darkness surrounded the fortress in which the earth had established its roots, creating a metallic wall in the midst of the vast sea. And at the entrance to this fortress stood the three Giants, ever vigilant, to guarantee tranquility to the gods.

The Meaning of the Myth

This myth expresses a familiar (or more precisely, *familial*), theme: conflict between the youthful protagonist and the father who fears that he will be overthrown. In his vain attempt to thwart this threat, the father assumes the figure of a tyrant, and does everything in his power to destroy his son/ rival.

There are other interesting details to this kind of story. There is usually the prophecy that the tyrant will finally be overthrown by a hero who had been abandoned at birth, either given up to the elements or ordered to be killed by domestic servants. While these details may vary somewhat from one version to another, their basic structure is clear and never changes: a great battle between the father/tyrant, and the son/ hero will take place. The significance of the relationship between the hero and his real mother, who usually assumes the risk of opposing the powerful father, is worth emphasizing. Indeed, she is often, though not always, the "brains" if not the "brawn" behind the reaping of vengeance against the father.

This collaboration between the son and the mother takes on its extreme form in the myth of Oedipus in which Destiny leads Oedipus to "involuntarily" kill the father and marry the mother. The individual act in this tragedy is conditioned by an external force such as "destiny" or the "will of the gods." Becker[7] has observed that the problem of life in this dual universe is to interpret and to control the power of the invisible and spiritual world. In the West, the belief in the dual universe has lasted from the Enlightenment up until the 19th century, after which it gradually diminished. In the 20th century, we think that all experience is real, all data are valid, and that we exist solely on the level of the visible world. But we must be mindful that the old concept of duality has lasted for over half a million years, while our new material view of the world is no more than one hundred and fifty years old.

This "reality principle" can be observed in its infancy in the literature of tragedy; in the representation of the father-son relationship in simple human terms; the displacement of intense conflict from outside to within the individual. The story of Hamlet, Prince of Denmark, which we will consider later in this book, is a magnificent example of this displacement. The aggressive forces of the hero/son are actually modelled on the persecutory designs of the paternal figure, and the entire complex is "projected" using mechanisms similar to those that produce dreams and psychoneurotic symptoms. Jones observes:[8]

> The elaboration of the more complex variants of the myth is brought about chiefly by three factors, namely; an increasing degree of distortion engendered by greater psychological "repression"; complication of the main theme by subsidiary allied ones; and an expansion of the story by repetition due to the creator's decorative fancy . . . The first and most important disturbing factor, that of more pronounced "repression" manifests itself by the same mechanism as those described by Freud in connection with normal dreams, psychoneurotic symptoms etc. The most interesting of these mechanisms is that known as "decomposition" . . . in which . . . various attributes of a given individual are disunited and several other individuals are invented, each endowed with one group of the original attributes . . . A great part of the Greek mythology must have arisen in this way. A good example of the process in the group now under consideration is seen by the figure of the tyrannical father becoming split into two, a father and a Tyrant . . . The resolution of the original figure is not complete, so that the two resulting figures stand in a close relationship to each other, being indeed, as a rule members of the same family. The Tyrant who seeks to destroy the hero is more commonly the grandfather, as in the legends of the heroes Cyrus, Gilgam, Perseus, Telephos and others, or the granduncle, as in those of Romulus and Remus and their Greek predecessors Amphion and Zethod. Less often is it the uncle as in the Hamlet and Brutus legends . . . When the decomposition is more complete, the Tyrant is not in the same family . . . (He) may be however apparently a complete stranger, as in the examples of Moses and the Pharaoh, Feridium and Zohak, Jesus and Herod, and others.

In short, the process of decomposition follows the gradual development of social organization from the simple beginning of the dispossessed father, to a more complicated arrangement among extended family members.

The fact that the human problems appear to be the same, but that the solutions to them differ in various cultures, has led to much research by students of mythology in an attempt to formulate general hypotheses concerning the realtionship between myth and rationality, and especially the content of the collective mind.

Origins of Punitive Society: Obedience and Reciprocity

In *The Punishment Response* (1978), Graeme Newman discussed the role of Freud's interpretation of the original myth of castration as it relates to punishment. The frame of reference used to flesh out two theoretical models of punishment were those of "reciprocity" and "obedience."[9]

Obedience contains the notions of transgression, deterrence, rules, and submission, while the model of reciprocity contains the notions of exchange equality and retribution.

It is clear that the myths we have described thus far may be seen as clear examples of the conflict of these two theoretical models. Reciprocity underlies the claims of the youthful revolutionary who perceives that he is being treated unjustly, and demands equality with the father (in no uncertain terms, in that he must sleep with the father's wife). At the same time, the obedience model underlies the father/tyrant's justification for his harsh actions against the son—for it is clear that it is not possible for the son actually to become his own father.

Each model is understandable as a moral justification for action. Obedience ensures stability of social order, makes everyday life predictable and secure. Reciprocity seeks to ensure that tyranny is not permitted, that each is treated equally. It is impossible for either of these models to be played out to its absolute end. An unavoidable paradox is involved because both models are equally justifiable moral claims to action. Little wonder that a "third party" (such as gods of various kinds, for example the Furies in the Orestia as we shall see in chapter 3) must be called upon to arbitrate. Indeed, this word is most appropriate, for it is only by an arbitrary judgment by a powerful third party that such an impossible conflict can be "resolved." It is the ultimate impossibility of its resolution, however, that produces the elementary sense of injustice.

The Elementary Sense of Injustice

Freud, "more than any other theorist of society, has shed light on the importance and power of myth, the fantastic capacity of man to symbolize his past."[10] He asserts that social organization and moral laws must have originated with the primal crime, a parricide. In the concluding chapter of *Totem and*

Taboo, Freud reconstructed the dynamics of the primal crime, the elements of which are clearly present in the myths that we have already discussed. But Freud adds that, after the crime, there followed the "totemic" feast in which the group came together in ritual to perform an animal sacrifice. Periodically, the totemic animal (substituted now for the original murdered father) would be killed and devoured. This act, still concrete in that an actual animal was killed and eaten, was nevertheless an important step in the direction of symbolizing the past, in making a symbolic substitution for the wish to fulfill the actual deed, which was that of killing and eating the father. Various anthropomorphic deities arose as a result of these practices, but one much more important psychological process arose during these rites.

The circumstance of killing and eating the totemic animal was performed by a group in solemn ritual. There was, according to Freud, a pervasive feeling of guilt because it was thought that the original crime was not justifiable if performed only by one individual; it could only be justified as a group action. The act was prohibited to single individuals, but was justified if all participated so that they could identify with each other through the totem.[11]

Freud drew on the Darwinian concept of the primordial condition of human society slowly developing from one in which there existed a horde, totally dominated by a tyrannical and jealous male leader, who took all the women to himself and cast aside all the sons. The next step in the development of social organization was for these sons to band together (the first notion of a "bond" in society) to overthrow the tyrannical father. In order to prevent the recurrent rising up of bands to overthrow each newly created "leader," the totemic ritual arose. The newly "bonded" band of young men established a system of "equal rights" among each other (the reciprocity model), but emphasized, some would say out of all proportion, submission and obedience to the totemic system, which perhaps ironically, became essentially matrilineal (the obedience model).[12]

The brothers' united effort put an end to the total domination of the father, but now they had to deal with their ambivalent feelings about this confrontation:

> They hated the father who stood so powerfully in the way of their sexual demands and their desire for power, but they also loved and

admired him. After they had satisfied their hate by his removal and had carried out their wish for identification with him, the suppressed tender impulses had to assert themselves. This took place in the form of remorse, a sense of guilt was formed which coincided here with remorse generally felt. The dead now became stronger than the living had been . . . What the father's presence had formerly prevented they themselves now formally prohibited.[13]

Not withstanding that the social bond was created to obtain liberty from oppression, the price paid to reach this objective was a horrible crime, which is, at bottom, the source of our cultural guilt. The subsequent rules and prohibitions (the first being incest) have, in actual fact, blocked this liberty. This is why we yearn for it, yet are unable to say exactly what it is that we want; except that it is a feeling of "having been put upon" that we wish to throw off. This is what we mean when we speak of the elementary sense of injustice. Essentially, its roots are in each individual's feeling of powerlessness and, at the same time, a yearning for power, and this feeling, in turn, is not related to one's position in the "social structure" (though it could exacerbate it), but rather to the fact that society exists at all.[14]

None of the sons obtained complete satisfaction from the "crime" they had committed. None in fact was able to obtain the complete supremacy that the original father had and to which all aspired. Through this veneration of the father, each individual came to recognize that he was distinct from other individuals (since the "bond" among them was not now directly between each of them, but only indirectly through the identification of the father). Thus, their ideal memory of the father created the idea of "god the father."

This was a crucial step, because heretofore, the primordial society had been, subsequent to the killing of the original father, dominated by the matriarchal line, which comes as no surprise when we consider the part played by the wife in the various myths we have described. But now, Freud says:

> With the insertion of the paternal divinity into the society which had been deprived of the father, society was gradually transformed into a patriarchical order. The family was the restoration of the old primitive order, and it also in large part restored the father's rights.[15]

Freud notes that society first treated kings as gods who transferred to the state the patriarchical system. We must be impressed by this unremitting process: the vengeance of the cast-down father now reinstated as the "authority figure" that we know so well.

Now we are able to define the origin of our social organization as one of incredible paradox: it lies in the crime of rebellion against "authority." A rebellion that was destined, because of the guilt produced by the crime, to reproduce authority over and over again. Out of this paradox probably developed all systems of regulation concerned with social order. With the act of rebellion the idea of obedience was born, producing its basic elements: the proliferation of rules, punishment, and submission.[16]

The model of obedience and the system of punishment that it seems to sustain, according to this view, is one of the oldest and most dominant systems of social control that serves to reinforce the fundamental institutions that society needs in order to survive. These basic institutions are comprised first and foremost of the family, later followed by religion, schools, and much later, a system of criminal justice.

The social order preceeding the original crime was constituted by a regime of pure violence, and it was by this single dimension of physical force that individuals were differentiated. At this time, there was no "obedience," but, as in the primal myth, only violence and fear. The crime of the brothers acting together brought a decentralization of the power structure—from the tyranny of one to the authority of many fathers. This new order displays a characteristic principle of social inequality: it is a social differentiation, indeed organization, based on the presupposition of an unequal distribution of authority. Not only was this system based on a certain consensus (the consensus implied by the brothers acting together as a group), but it also depended on a system of punishments, for it is essentially through punishment that authority manifests itself.

The Origins of a Vengeful Culture:
The Animistic Basis of Reciprocity

Reciprocal exchange has an undeniable animistic side to it. It originates in the ancient relationship between primeval man and nature, a period preceeding the creation of any social order. During that period, man was immersed in an unpredictable and hostile world, which, for various reasons,[17] contributed to the primitive conception of an animated nature, the attribution of intentionality to the natural world. Man was, in fact, part of nature itself, and in this way developed a sense of responsibility for "mistakes" that occurred in nature, such as floods and droughts. Consequently, he felt a sense of "guilt" and developed many religious rites designed to ensure that nature would treat him well. This magical quality of "give and take" between man and the natural world, leads easily to endowing a magical quality to all exchanges, whether material or not, whether with nature of with other men.

However, if the idea of exchange or reciprocity was born in the deep recesses of ancient society, in the void between Man and Nature, one might ask whether the notion of obedience was not also born in the same way, especially as it was a popular view of the savage by nineteenth century anthropologists that he was a "slave" to nature. We will see in the next chapter that it is very likely that the demands of obedience, if they did not preceed those of reciprocity as Durkheim suggested, have certainly superceded them.[18] Indeed, primitive man was more used to threats than are we. He knew very well that Nature could punish him mercilessly.

We see, then, that there are good reasons for man's having committed the primal crime, in one version or the other, as recounted in the Greek myths. But there are also equally good reasons why the "crime" became a crime—that is, it was imbued with the essential element of modern day crime—guilt. And we also see why the crime was followed by what can be described as nothing other than cleansing rituals, that is, a plethora of rules and prohibitions, and a subsequent slavish submission to their every letter.

We must remember that these are largely imaginary reconstructions of the beginnings of social order. We can only guess at the "true" basis of the beginnings of society. There were probably, in actual fact, many primal crimes, and many separate societies formed. It is also possible that society could have developed in a different direction. We are inclined to take the side of natural science in proposing that society took the direction it did as a result of chance; in this instance, the fortunate discovery of the power of tools and weapons.[19] The Freudians are more convinced that the reason for violence being at the core of society is man's base instinct. Fromm, in his *Anatomy of Human Destructiveness*, catalogs and describes a number of societies (admittedly very much in the minority) that appear to be based on love and altruism. However, since it is patently clear that the essential core of Western society is not love (in the ideal sense of that word), it is appropriate to give more importance to the Freudian analysis. We must repeat, it is not so much that this analysis tells of the "true" beginning of society, but that it does lend credence to the constructions that have arisen to explain the beginning of culture.

It is in the nature of myths to consolidate or condense the particulars of many past occurrences into one general story. They are, in this way, a highly saturated version of huge historical periods. Nevertheless, we are able to observe in these myths, a clear development and refinement over the ages, especially in relation to the process of punishment. In this respect, they begin with stories of atrocious retaliations, and progress to later recountings of early social organizations, especially the family within which the primal crime for the first time established a respect for authority, eventually leading to the now well established patriarchal system of western society. In this way, the family has avoided internal conflict. Each social group has learned that authority must be respected, or the group will die.

Thus, in the primitive family born out of the dissolution of the primal "order," obedience was owed first to the father (and initially by the father to his mother), and second to the rules of the totemic system. As families and clans developed, they became more diversified and a variety of complex kinship organizations arose. However, we can see that the reciprocity model has become more and more atrophied, but the original "cause" nevertheless lies in the background and underlies all authority structures, exhibiting itself as a yearning for freedom, the quest for equality. The demand for reciprocity lies at the bottom of the question asked by all great sociologists from Durkheim to Merton: why do men obey?

The yearning for reciprocity is as close as we can come to defining in a positive sense what it is that men want. It is as close as we can come to defining justice. Yet we see that not only is such a conception of justice based on a biological impossibility—the wish to be one's own father, but that its motivations are suspect. It is a concept of justice full of resentment. Of course, the wish for reciprocity is never expressed in such crass Freudian terms by our modern day revolutionaries. Instead, they preach that we must take control of our own destinies, that we must be totally free from the domination of man by man. Such catch-cries for "freedom" we now understand, and recognize their ambiguity. We know that the "freedom" that comes after any revolution simply reproduces, in the new society, a system of domination similar to that of the myths we have described in this chapter.

Therefore, we consider ourselves to be on safer ground by avoiding the concept of justice altogether, and instead developing the concept of the elementary sense of injustice, because we know the exact origin of this sense, and what it represents. Although the idea of reciprocity comes close to the idea of justice that revolutionaries and conservatives stand for, it is nevertheless difficult to see why, in the sphere of punishment, returning one wrong for another is either necessarily or inherently "just," yet this is what is assumed by the reciprocity model, and it is *the* ingredient of the idea of vengeance, and its modern day counterpart, retribution.

Summary

1. The two models of reciprocity and obedience are clearly in conflict. The obedience model presupposes structural inequality between those who impose obedience and those who suffer it. But there is also an assumption underlying this model that there is the possibility—indeed, if we are to be guided by the great myths of culture—the inevitability that those held in obedience do not want to be so. That is, there is a recognition that the reciprocity model lies hidden, ready to rise up at the right moment and put an end to obedience. For the reciprocity model, we have seen, presupposes a basic equality in social position in each party.

2. We may say that the social order is essentially a dynamic order, and the force of this dynamic derives from the fundamental cultural conflict between the obedience model that remains always visible and heavy-handed, and the more hidden model of reciprocity that lies quietly, only showing itself indirectly in the form of feuds with other clans in which each side is deemed to be equal in social position, or in obsessions with the establishment of systems of "justice" that are aimed at defending the "weak."

3. Examples of reciprocity include feuding subcultures that may be interpreted as attempts to maintain social order without resorting to the obedience model. To those of us who are used to "obedient" societies, we view such "order" as chaos. We will examine such feuding societies in chapter 6.

4. Examples of the attempt to establish systems of "justice," are the basic tenets of Mosaic law and their variations: the talion principle (as Freud termed it), or *lex talionis*, the law of retribution (an eye for an eye, a tooth for a tooth). This law demands that a wrong must be punished by a wrong of equal proportion and kind. We can see clearly the coercive basis of both models; we can also see that the moral claims of vengeance or retribution are not much more than elaborate excuses to seize power. Viewed in this light, vengeance is seen as an obsession with the power of an instinct, especially in its infantile and elementary stage, and in its advanced form, becomes a cultural process with the psychological attributes of a neurosis.

Notes

1. Sigmund Freud. "Creative Writers and Day-dreaming." In *The Standard Edition of the Complete Works of Sigmund Freud*. Trans. James Strachey (London: Hogarth Press, 1964) p. 152.

2. He describes a myth of the Hittites (a race of people existing around 2000 years B.C.) and their traditional enemy the Horites (an indo-european race distributed throughout western Asia). In this story, Kumarbi overthrows the god of the sky, Anu, by biting off his penis and swallowing it. He becomes pregnant by the powerful god of the storms (a parallel to Zeus), god of the sky and the seasons. The details are so similar to the Greek version that they probably derived from the same model. See G. S. Kirk, *La Natura dei Miti Greci* (Bari: Laterza, 1980) p. 119.

3. Ibid, p. 294.

4. C. G. Jung, *Man and his Symbols* (New York: Doubleday, 1964).

5. In the following passages we have relied heavily on the classic works of K. Kerényi, *Gli Dei e gli Eroi della Grecia* (Milano: Garzanti, 1978, vol. 1), p. 24–30.

6. Throughout the book, we have used the Greek terminology in naming the gods, with some exceptions if it seemed that the more common name was the Latin version.

7. E. Becker, *The Birth and Death of Meaning* (New York: The Free Press, 1971), p. 120.

8. E. Jones, *Hamlet and Oedipus* (Garden City, N.J.: Doubleday, 1954), pp. 149 f.

9. These models may best be conceived of as "ideal functions" of

punishment, after the manner in which Weber spoke of ideal types. In other words, it is likely that no particlar act of punishment in real life represents purely one or the other function. Rather, the two functions will always be mixed.

10. G. R. Newman, *The Punishment Response* (Philadelphia: Lippincott, 1978).

11. S. Freud, *Totem and Taboo*, trans. A. A. Brill (New York: Random House, 1918) passim.

12. Ibid.

13. *Totem and Taboo*, pp. 184–85.

14. We may say that this observation applies significantly to Marx who was most able in saying what was wrong, at pointing to injustices due to class differentiation, but was considerably vague and ambiguous when it came to stating precisely what the state of being liberated would feel like, or even what kind of society it would engender.

15. *Totem and Taboo*, pp. 186–87.

16. The crime of rebellion, probably the most serious of all crimes, was stigmatized in the religious tradition of many peoples, and is known as original sin. Its secular form is treason—the worst offense.

17. Newman, *The Punishment Response*, chap. 2.

18. E. Durkheim, *The Elementary Forms of Religious Life* (New York: The Free Press, 1965).

19. We suggest this thesis after the movie *2001*, in which an ape discovers that he can kill much more easily using a large bone as a club.

2

Vengeance as Anger

For I have no desire myself to live and remain among men, unless I
may kill Hector first with my own spear.
> —Achilles upon hearing that his good friend,
> Patrocles, had been killed by Hector.[1]

The Wrath of Achilles

THE ENTIRE ILIAD EXPRESSES the wrath of Achilles. Homer tells
many stories about the final phases of the Trojan war, but
wrathful sentiment underlies the development and resolution
of action from the initial conflict with Agememnon to the
consummation of vengeance in the killing of Hector.

In the first verses of the epic, the Muse of poetry, Calliope, is
invoked to sing of "the bitter rancour of Achilles . . . which
brought a thousand troubles upon the [Greeks]."[2]

The events of the Iliad take place on the plain around the
fortified city of Troy, whose walls were said to have been built
by the god Apollo somewhere between 1260 and 1300 B.C.
Agamemnon, king of Argos and Mycenae and commander of
the Greek army, beseiged the fortified city for almost ten years.
The official "cause" of the war was to avenge the offense on
Agamemnon's brother Menelaus, whose wife, Helen, had been
abducted and taken to Troy by Paris, son of the Trojan king,
Priam.[3] The events leading up to the Trojan war are widely
reported in the mythological tradition,[4] and are often referred
to throughout the Iliad.

24

The real action begins when the chiefs of the Greek army assemble to discuss a very serious problem. After ten years of war, plague had spread throughout the camp, killing many soldiers and placing the entire operation in question. (The reader knows why this plague has descended on the camp: Apollo was upset because Agamemnon had refused to liberate his slave girl Chryseis, the daughter of Chryse priest of the god, even though he had offered to pay an appropriate ransom.)

The assembly is addressed by Achilles, son of the goddess Thetis and of the mortal Peleus. Achilles was said to be invulnerable because his mother, as soon as he was born, held him by the heel and immersed him in the river Styx. (Whoever was wet by the waters of this underground stream became invulnerable.) The heel was not wet by the magic water, and so remained the only vulnerable part of the hero's body. Achilles proposed to ask the prophet Calchas ("the son of Testor, the greatest of the prophets, who knew the present the past and the future,"[5]) why Apollo was punishing their military exercise so severely, and how to placate his anger. Calchas spoke, saying that he knew the answer, but before he could give the explanation, he must have the protection of Achilles because his words could be very unpleasant to a very important man who may wish to punish him. Achilles immediately assured him that, as long as he, Achilles, lived, no one would dare to do him evil because of his revelations. "No one," Achilles affirmed, "not even if it were Agamemnon who now boasts that he is the strongest of us all."[6]

Calchas, encouraged by these words, explained that the revenge of the god was caused by the offenses done towards his priest, and that this revenge would not end unless Chryseis were returned to her father without payment of any ransom. This act of obedience must be accompanied by the ritual sacrifice of one hundred cows. Agamemnon, suddenly called on by the prophet, was forced to stand up and declare that he would restore the girl and fulfill the ritual of expiation, if this was what was needed to end the plague. However, his speech was full of hostility against Calchas, and highly provocative to the chiefs of the other armies. He announced that, in fact, he expected to be repaid for the loss of Chryseis, since as chief of the Greek army, he had no intention of going without his share of the booty. Achilles, who had controlled his own hot temper so far, pointed out that the gifts of booty from the conquered city had already been shared, and that it would be appropriate for Agamemnon to temporarily renounce his claims, and later receive his share, perhaps even more, once the city of Troy was conquered. Agamemnon, however, reasserted his intention to strip some of the chiefs, perhaps Achilles himself, of their booty.

The discussion between the two leaders following these repeated threats, led to an open conflict. Achilles was not disposed to submit to the provocation of anyone. He knew that he was probably the strongest of the heroes participating in the expedition, and that the outcome of the war could depend on him. (Mythological and literary sources all agree on Achilles' exceptional strength, courage, and speed.) He upbraided Agamemnon, insulting him, reminding him that the principal reason for the expedition was to vindicate the offense made against Agamemnon's brother, Menalaus. Furthermore, he argued, since Agamemnon would now provide no recognition of the merits of the other chiefs, he, along with his faithful followers, would abandon the enterprise.

Agamemnon replied angrily that he had no interest in whether Achilles stayed with him or not, and, furthermore, in order to show just how powerful he was, he would take his booty by force. This was the slave Briseis who had been obtained by Achilles according to common agreement after the sacking of the city of Lyrnessos.[7]

The conflict between the two leaders came to a critical point. Agamemnon did not seem to realize just how far he could go in provoking Achilles, whose anger had brought him to the brink of murder. Achilles was about to draw his sword when the goddess Athena intervened in order to avert the worst.[8]

She stopped Achilles, asking him not to kill his rival, promising him that he would one day be rewarded for this renunciation. Achilles resentfully obeyed her divine wish. "So he stayed his heavy hand on the silver hilt, and drove back the sword into the sheath."[9] At this point, the conflict seemed unresolvable. Achilles would not fight any more for the common cause, and for this reason many would die. While Ulysses went to Chryse to make the sacrifice and give back the daughter, Agamemnon sent two emissaries to Achilles' tent to steal away his slave Briseis. Achilles withdrew, smoldering over the injustice done to him. Immediately, his mother Thetis rose from the depths of the sea, and promised to convince Zeus to favor the Trojans, so that after suffering serious casualties, Agamemnon would realize what a serious error he had committed in humiliating her son.

Vengeance and the Common Bond:
The Ambiguity of Authority

The conflict betwen the two heroes is the thrust of the entire epic. It is the wrath of Achilles that, along with vengeance, constitutes the main theme of the poem. Indeed, the two themes are so tightly bound that they may well comprise the most uniquely creative aspect of the poem.[10]

This lengendary conflict is often depicted as one in which the "heroes" partook in a grand war. But in reality, these heroic leaders were chiefs of small primitive communities, bound together to carry out a typically punitive expedition, motivated mostly by the quest for booty. It must be clear, however, that the social bonds within this community of relatives and friends were not bonds of vassals to lords—that is, there was no set hierarchical structure.[11] These leaders, with regard to one another, were in a position of reciprocity and independence, society not yet having developed a feudal or monarchic structure.[12]

During this period, public power or law did not exist, nor even a system of sanctions administered by an authority as an external protagonist. The absence of this power, and the custom of taking important decisions to a primitive assembly (where everybody keeps his rights and tries to impose his will according to purely individual interests), is at the source of Agamemnon's contradictory behavior. On one hand, he has the power to deprive Achilles of his booty, but on the other, he cannot force Achilles to continue to fight for him. Thus we see a curious fluctuation of power and impotence.[13] He is called "the leader of the Greeks," but "to be a real king he lacks the most important thing, namely, who could save him if Athena had not stopped Achilles' arm as it extracted the sword?"[14]

The authority of Agamemnon was not formalized or permanent, but was based on voluntary agreement among the leaders, each of whom was a sovereign.[15] It should be clear that, in the Iliad, each time someone has the duty to participate in the war, this duty is meant to refer to the duty of the sovereign to himself and to his own people.[16] This agreement could be revoked at any time, and possibly turn into a conflict that would result in a feud. Order was therefore constantly problematic.

Order from Above: Vengeance and Divine Intervention

Athena's intervention broke the normal evolution of the conflict. Achilles' contained aggression was the beginning of the process that today we call repression. It was now possible for Achilles to displace his anger from its natural object and direct it toward substitute objects, namely Hector and the "Trojan enemies." Thus, the opposite result was achieved; instead of the Greeks losing the war without Achilles, they would gain from his redirected energy.

The role of the gods in the Iliad is more complex than that described in the myth of castration in chapter 1, since the social organization has become more complex. The original rebellion among the gods on Mount Olympus brought a decentralization of the power structure from the tyranny of one to the authority of many fathers. This "new order" displays the characteristic principle of social inequality, the basis of the obedience model.

But in the Iliad, while the gods still intervene, the responsibility to maintain order falls more and more upon mortals because basic differences between men and gods are recognized. Gods cannot take their threats of punishment to the extreme since they are, by definition, all powerful, and therefore cannot be subject to coercion beyond a certain point. They cannot die; at most they suffer limited and often ridiculous sanctions. The result is that, when Zeus hears something said against him by his wife and children, he raises his voice often but does not control the situation as well as Agamemnon. Zeus must deal with gods after all; Agamemnon with mere mortals. So on earth, within the clans, a certain form of authority was probably recognized—most probably in the arena of battle rather than within families, at least if we judge from the sad story of Agamemnon, killed, as we shall see, by his vengeful wife. In contrast, the interclan relationships appear to be widely regulated by the norm of reciprocity.

However, the new order, while based on a degree of collective consent, was not stable, given the minimal social regulation of conflict due to the continuous reassertion of the need for reciprocity, which in this case had expressed itself through the force of Achilles' wrath.

Thus we see that vengeance, in the early stages of its "civilization" appears as a wrathful force, barely controlled at the social level, yet tending towards "self regulation." The situation is precarious because vengeance tends to upset the delicate balance between obedience and reciprocity. "Real" order does not exist. Nor does "justice." The idea of the latter will appear only in the tragedy described in the next chapter.

Decomposition of the Sense of Injustice

We are able to interpret this drama as an evolutionary development of the hero/tyrant conflict referred to in the preceeding chapter. In this case, we see a confrontation between a young hero [Achilles] who is threatened by a tyrannical and unreasonable power represented by Agamemnon. The relationship between the two is not one of subordination, but is more reciprocal, in the sense that, the outcome of the conflict could favor Achilles. However, Agamemnon is, at least formally, king of the Greeks. It is said that, "he gives orders to more men,"[17] and Achilles seems more or less to vaguely feel the influence of Agamemnon's authority. This expresses a complex psychological relationship between the two heroes that has its origin in the distant past.

It is worth noting that a latent conflict between the two heroes is already discernible in the episode concerning Calchas' prophecy when he invokes the protection of Achilles. At that moment Achilles states that not even Agamemnon, who is supposed to be the most powerful, could hurt the prophet with impunity. During the subsequent discussion, it is clear that Achilles' hatred has its origin in the intention of Agamemnon to keep all the advantages of the expedition for himself. The crucial point of the controversy revolves around Achilles' insistence that the booty be shared "equitably." This means that Achilles feels very keenly an elementary sense of injustice, an undeniable sense of feeling deprived and oppressed. Achilles openly expressed this psychological condition with these words: "I feel bitter grief in my heart when here is a man who will rob his equal and take back his prize because he is the stronger."[18] The sense of injustice felt by Achilles has an immediate effect on his wish to retaliate, a wish only just controlled by divine intervention. His wrath was contained in this way until the conditions arose for the accomplishment of vengeance. We may also note that, where Achilles' wrath had its origin in the relationship between father and son, the two protagonists in the Iliad were not presented as part of the same family, but instead as complete strangers. This is due to the process of "decomposition" that we have described in the preceding chapter, so that Agamemnon was no longer recognized as a real father. As Jones argues,[19]

> "It is clear that this scale of increasing decomposition from an actual father to an apparently complete stranger . . . corresponds with—and is doubtless due to—further stages of repression; the more repressed is the idea that the father is a hateful tyrant, the more completely is the imaginàry figure of the persecuting tyrant dissociated from the recognized father."

In the Iliad, the social body appears articulated into groups or clans, which, as the prelude to the Odyssey, suggests the beginning of an evolution from a primitive democracy toward an aristocracy and monarchy. While the social bond is step-by-step articulated in more and more complex forms, the prevalence of the model of obedience seems to become greater. At the same time, the quest for equality and reciprocity is more and more deeply buried, but is never forgotten.

To continue the story, Achilles withdrew, sulking in his tent, deprived "arbitrarily" of his beloved slave and publicly humiliated by Agamemnon. But the battle for the conquest of Troy continued and for a large part of the poem, little more is said about the wrath of Achilles or of vengeance.

When the defeat that was anticipated (due to the intervention of Zeus upon the request of his mother Thetis) came dangerously close, a group of "ambassadors" approached Achilles with the hope of appeasing him. The ambassadors were led by Ulysses, the most astute of the Greek heroes, who tried to induce Achilles to accept Agamemnon's apologies. Although these apologies were offered together with the return of his slave Briseis and some other gifts, Achilles scorned the offers, conceding that only when Hector, the Trojan leader, should be close to threatening him, his men or property, "will (Achilles) know how to stop him."[20]

Very soon, this feared event arrived. The battle moved near the ships, the destruction of which would impede the army's ability to escape. At this point, Achilles' best friend Patrocles, moved to compassion at the sad fate of the other warriors, asked the stubborn Achilles to at least let him wear his arms and participate in the battle so that the Trojans, believing Achilles himself to have returned to the field, would draw back, giving a respite to the Greek army.

Achilles agreed, since it allowed him to maintain his promise not to participate directly in the battle, and also, we may assume, because the sight of the destruction of the Greeks had partly softened his desire for vengeance. However, he urged Patrocles to limit himself to drawing the enemy away from the ships and the encampment, and not to try reaching the wall of the city. (It will be remembered that the walls of Troy were said to be sacred to the god Apollo).

Patrocles did not follow his friend's advice. He pushed the Trojans further and further back until he reached the top of the wall. Apollo himself was forced to intervene: "Get back, Patrocles," he said, "It is not destined for the city to fall under your lance, nor is it destined for the proud Trojans to fall under the lance of Achilles, who is so much stronger than you."[21]

But Patrocles' fate was already decided. The angry god made his helmet fall in the dust and Hector immediately inflicted a mortal wound. As Patrocles lay dying, he responded to Hector's boasting, by pointing out that he also would not have a long life, for he could never escape the vengeance of Achilles. All day long the battle raged around the body of Patrocles for his companions did not want to leave it to the enemy.

Meanwhile, Achilles heard of the death of his friend. His grief was so great, that all were afraid that he would kill himself. But the need for vengeance directed him away from self-destruction. He would not bury Patrocles before he had killed Hector and had sacrificed twelve sons of noble Trojans in front of the funeral pyre. We see that then, as today, it was not enough to repay equally what had been done, but rather to demand something more. Achilles prepared for the final battle, well aware that the killing of Hector would shortly precede his own death, since this was his Destiny. His own life was not worth continuing if he could not avenge Patrocles' death.

Achilles rapidly made a formal appeasement with Agamemnon. (This stage of the poem is known as the "interruption of the wrath of Achilles," showing the process of displacement of anger from its original object, Agamemnon, to Hector and the Trojans). Agamemnon made the excuse that he "wasn't himself" when he offended Achilles. "Zeus took away my mind," he said.[22] Thus, Agamemnon was no longer recognized as the real object of vengeance; it was now Hector who, in reality, was a "casual" killer, guided by the hand of Apollo.

The final part of the Iliad describes the slaughter of the Trojans by Achilles in his effort to reach Hector. During the battle, the powerful force of Achilles' anger burst forth, and vengeance was directed indiscriminately towards all the enemy. Achilles spared no lives; showed no mercy, not even to those who pleaded for their lives. Had Patrocles lived, he would have shown mercy, as he had done in the past, but now, only death, even his own death, could make up for the death of his friend.

Eventually, he caught up to Hector and they prepared for the final battle. Hector said that he would return Achilles' body to the Greeks, should he win, and asked Achilles if he would do the same for him. Achilles refused all conditions: how could there be an agreement between them? At this moment, Hector had to demonstrate all his prowess and courage but his fate had already been decided. After a brief fight, Achilles slew him with his lance. And while Hector lay dying, Achilles reminded him of the killing of Patrocles, for which he had foolishly thought he would go unpunished. He then tied the body to his chariot and dragged it away.

The poem is near its conclusion. Achilles has only to give his friend a proper burial, and then await his own death. Yet, in spite of his threats not to return Hector's body, he agrees, in the end, to return it in response to the pleas of Hector's father, Priam. The thirst for vengeance was at last extinguished.

The story of the death of Achilles does not belong to the Iliad. According to tradition, he was later killed by an arrow shot by Paris, whose hand was guided by Apollo. The arrow hit Achilles in the heel. No mortal could have killed him in open battle. His bones rest in a tomb, "on a promontory on the coast, just at the entrance of the Hellespont, so high that sailors at any time could see it from a great distance.[23]

Mastering the Force

The permanent and enduring need for reciprocity is clearly demonstrated in the Iliad. The need is so strong that vengeance, at this stage, is still an absolute duty, with the force of an instinct, and is more powerful than the need for survival. Vengeance must be done, even though it will cost the avenger his life. We still see this today, for example, the suicide bombings of modern terrorists. The ideological reasons for retaliation may have become more complex, but the basic psychological mechanisms, now thousands of years old, remain the same.

Another characteristic of vengeance at this stage is that it expresses itselfs as nonspecific aggression. This lack of specificity underlies the primitive element of the noncontainment of the aggressive drive that "suffers badly" the progress towards order and civilization. During this process, aggression, although found within a retributive logic, becomes a little more subject to rational control. That is, in the first stage in the maturation of vengeance, there is an attempt to give a *reason* for carrying out vengeance: it is not a completely automatic or spontaneous act.

In Homer, man is still not the complete master of his own actions, nor of the reality that surrounds him. He is not yet completely separated from nature and therefore does not possess the necessary precondition for abstract thinking. He is still prey to external forces. The "divine apparatus" used in the Iliad to convey this external force is expressed by the intervention of the divinities in the lives of the protagonists during the entire story. The gods, in fact, appear in human form, and tend to think like humans. An important characteristic of the Greek "culture" was that men's actions became progressively less determined by the will of the gods.

In fact Achilles has not yet developed a total concept of the self. This was, according to classical scholars, typical of the Hellenic period.[24] But throughout the epic, we do see Achilles' personality evolve towards greater autonomy, since he comes to assume personal responsibility in accepting his own death as the price for taking vengeance. Although he is probably the prototype of the "well-connected" half-god (that is, invulnerable but rash and irresponsible), at the crucial moment when he makes the decision to take vengeance at the price of his own life, he asserts his humanity by rationalizing that, as one of the "ruling class," he must kill Hector because it is his duty as a chief who is responsible for the lives of his warriors. In this way, he gives meaning to his actions.

The self-destructive forces related to his raw impulses are nevertheless still too strong, and do not allow for the formation of a more mature psychological character, capable of channeling these forces towards instrumental goals more suited to the changing individual and collective conditions of survival. This kind of character is only sketched in by Homer in the Iliad, but in the Odyssey, it is more fully defined. It is to this story that we now turn for the next step in the "maturation" of vengeance.

Notes

1. Homer, The Iliad, trans. W. H. D. Rouse (New York: Mentor, Book XVIII) p. 217.

2. Ibid, Book I, p. 11.

3. See note 4.

4. As we saw in the preceding chapter, after Zeus took power from the "chtonic" divinities, a kind of patriarchical regime was established. That same Zeus became father of a number of Olympian gods who were said to have lived in a house on mount Olympus. These divinities had close ties with many mortals.

5. Omero, Iliade (Milano: Mondadori, 1977) Book I, vv. 69–70, our translation.

6. Ibid., Book I, vv. 90–91, p. 27, our translation.

7. During the nine years that preceded the events narrated in the Iliad, the Greek expedition had conquered several cities, among which were Lyrnessos. It was common for the women to be shared among the victors.

8. "Minerva came from the Heavens," says Homer, "and Achilles was struck breathless, immediately recognizing her, and his eyes flashed wildly." Ibid, Book I, vv. 194–200, p. 30, our translation.

9. The Iliad, Book I, p. 15.

10. P. Manzon, "Struttura e genesi dell' Iliade," ed. F. Codino, La Questione Omerica (Roma: Editori, Riuniti 1976), p. 145.

11. F. Codino, "Prefazione all' Iliade", in Omero, Iliade, p. 11.

12. This archaic context is noticeable in many other respects: the army is small, although according to the usual amplification of the epic, Agamemnon is said to have commanded 120,000 men; the army does not have a board of officials, nor does it display a true military structure. Ibid, pp. 11–12.

13. G. Jachmann, "I poteri di Agamemnnone: finzione e realtà", ed F. Codino, *La Questione Omerica*, p. 126.

14. Codino, "Prefazione all' Iliade", p. 13.

15. G. Jachmann, "I poteri", p. 127. Weber has examined this question in considerable detail. See M. Weber, "Politics as a Vocation" in H. Gerth, and C. W. Mills, *From Max Weber* (New York: Oxford, 1968). The sovereign must be legitimated or charismatic before obedience can be guaranteed. And even then it is uncertain.

16. G. Jachman, "I poteri", p. 127.

17. Ibid., p. 128.

18. *The Iliad*, Book XVI, p. 188.

19. See E. Jones, *Hamlet and Oedipus* (Garden City N.Y.: Doubleday, 1954), p. 151.

20. *Iliade*, Book IX, v. 655, p. 184.

21. *Iliade*, Book XVI, vv. 701–709, p. 318, our death and to repay the Cyclops for its aggression. Vengeance is the instrument used to solve Ulysses' immediate problem of being put to death, and to later kill the princes for having usurped his throne.

The Cyclops is first defeated by words. Ulysses says that his name is "no one," assuming that the simple giant would associate a word directly with a person, unable to separate it as a concept. Thus, when Ulysses blinds the giant and the other giants ask who had done this deed, he replies, "No one."

Ulysses adopts a plan that will liberate him from the monster: he will offer it wine, and then, taking advantage of its drunkenness, will blind it with a red hot stick thrust into the one eye in the middle of its forehead. The next day, when the Cyclops comes to shift the huge stone from the only entrance to its cave, he and his companions will escape by hanging under the bellies of sheep.

3

From Vengeance to Justice

"[Ulysses] . . . lay wide awake, pondering his plans of vengeance."
—*The Odyssey*[1]

The Astute Ulysses

THE STORY OF THE VOYAGES of Ulysses to which we now turn is also the story of the growth of human character. Ulysses' vengeance against the princes of Ithaca is to become his self-fulfilment.

After ten years, with the war of Troy at an end, each surviving hero has returned to his home. But Ulysses, whose creative genius had produced the great wooden horse that made the conquest of Troy possible, was unable to return directly home to his waiting wife Penelope and son Telemacus, now an adult. Ulysses had been away from Ithaca for about twenty years, and during that time, the remaining princes had arrogantly set themselves up in his home, aspiring to marry his wife and take his place as king.

The Odyssey is the story of Ulysses' voyage home. His goal is to restore the "status quo" (which had been changed by the arrogance of the pretenders), and to restore himself as king. His tool is vengeance. "Ulysses must return in order to inflict on the would-be usurpers of his throne the punishment that they deserve." said Zeus.[2]

Preparing for Vengeance

The most prominent traits that define the actions of Ulysses are intelligence, and cunning, that is the use of knowledge to control and manipulate nature and other men. In this respect, Ulysses probably represents the first "modern" and psychologically structured character in western literature. We will see that his maturation coincides with the fulfilment of vengeance.

In the Iliad, Ulysses does not display these characteristics very clearly, although his role as a subtle mediator is emphasized in several places in the epic. According to the legend, both his parents were descended from gods, and he was, in fact, the son of Sisiphos who had twice tricked death. Such credentials make him one of the more astute personalities in antiquity. However, Sisyphus' punishment for this trickery shows the uselessness of trying to escape the common destiny of mortals: he was condemned forever to push a huge rock up hill, which when it neared the top, rolled down again.[3]

In spite of his distinguished family tree and his proverbial intelligence, Ulysses was, for seven years, kept on the island of the nymph Calypso who kept him there against his will, promising him eternal life. Eventually, he was allowed to leave, but on his way to Ithaca, his raft was destroyed by a furious sea stirred up by the hand of his enemy, the god Poseidon. Luckily, he managed to reach the island of the Phaiacian people, and at the court of Alcinous, he told of his adventures during his voyage after the conquest of Troy. These "vicissitudes" constitute the central part of the Odyssey. They "prepare" Ulysses for regaining his power and for the reunion with his family.

The monsters and enchanted situations that Ulysses encountered during his voyage on the Mediterranean are basically threats to his self-preservation.[4] His strategy is, where appropriate, to avoid, to attack, or to negotiate, always with a view to neutralize the threats. To do this, he must understand the phenomena that face him. These forces continually attempt to annihilate his ego, which, through the course of the journey, tries to achieve an "objective" and "instrumental" conception of the world. They are forces left from his infancy and, in a more general way, from the primitive past. For an undeveloped ego, the forces are incomprehensible in their violence, but when "decoded" by the advanced ego, they dissolve, and with them the fear or the darkness of the past from which the forces are derived. For this to happen, the ego must be separated from the world, and must consider it as an

object. In other words, before Ulysses can be master of his
realm and of his family, he must first be master of himself. The
sacrifice he must pay for this power is separation from the
world, and delay in the satisfaction of immediate needs. That
is, he must be ready to "renounce" immediate gratification in
order to achieve future satisfaction that becomes, by definition, a symbolic reward. This process, only sketchily drawn in
the Iliad, underlies the entire action of the Odyssey. The
adventures threaten the life of the hero and his companions;
they also tempt him to give up the struggle and fall back into
his primitive state. This regression to a former state means the
annihilation of his ego. For example, he almost loses his life in
a confrontation with the Cyclops; and almost regresses into a
vegetative, animal-like state in his encounter with Circe
whose magical powers overwhelm him. His visit to the island
of the Cyclops shows most completely the conflict between
uncontrollable and terrifying forces, and the rational development of the ego.

The First Use of Cunning

The Cyclopes are a very primitive tribe of monsters, living
with only a semblance of social regulation. The one-eyed giant
who imprisons Ulysses and his companions in the cave and
starts to eat them systematically, is subject to no law. The
giant's thought is simple and disordered, all the time prey to
his primordial impulses. Ulysses' vengeance is part of his
strategy to avoid death and to repay the Cyclops for its
aggression. Vengeance is the instrument used to solve Ulysses'
immediate problem of being put to death, and to later kill the
princes for having usurped his throne.

The Cyclops is first defeated by words. Ulysses says that his
name is "no one," assuming that the simple giant would
associate a word directly with a person, unable to separate it
as a concept. Thus, when Ulysses blinds the giant and the
other giants ask who had done this deed, he replies, "No one."

Ulysses adopts a plan that will liberate him from the monster: he will offer it wine, and then, taking advantage of its
drunkenness, will blind it with a red hot stick thrust into the
one eye in the middle of its forehead. The next day, when the
Cyclops comes to shift the huge stone from the only entrance

to its cave, he and his companions will escape by hanging under the bellies of sheep.

Ulysses' actions demonstrate a number of important psychological features. First, he was able to renounce the immediate gratification of vengeance against the Cyclops. He could have simply killed the giant while it was sleeping, especially as it had already eaten two of his companions. But Ulysses waited, for fear that he would be trapped in the cave, since nobody could move the huge rock at its entrance. So he paused, evaluated the situation, and adopted a plan that would allow him to attain both goals: vengeance, and the preservation of his own life: "I was left brooding and full of dark plans, longing to have my revenge, if only Athena would grant my prayer."[5] His ability to delay gratification of his impulses and to consider reality in an objective manner in order to survive are the distinguishing characteristics of Ulysses' actions. We may regard this as a "preliminary trial" for the ultimate solution against the pretenders to his throne. Vengeance, in these circumstances, is delayed, and in fact becomes far more effective when finally carried out. It is the beginning of a utilitarian motive for vengeance. (A utilitarian use of vengeance is taken to its logical extreme by the Mafia, as we will see in chapter 9).

However, vengeance still remains the "natural" solution to the conflict, without any consideration of its legitimacy. Indeed, from the bridge of his ship at the moment of escape, Ulysses could not resist addressing the Cyclops in derisive tones. In this single moment, he risked being hit by rocks that the giant was throwing blindly in the direction of his voice. It was an impulse that Ulysses could not forgo because it gave him so much psychological satisfaction.

This is one of the early adventures of the Odyssey, and the day of return is still far away. He has many miraculous escapes from death, thanks to the combination of his personal qualities and divine help.

Careful Consummation

Ulysses landed at Ithaca where a difficult situation awaited him. The pretenders had taken over his home, acting as if they were the owners. They outnumbered him, so they could not be defeated by a direct attack. In order to carry out vengeance, Ulysses had to make himself stronger, and try to bring about more favourable conditions for an attack.

Shortly after his arrival in a deserted area of the island, there occurred the first of a number of meetings with Athena, his protector. She gave encouragement to Ulysses who seemed to be perplexed in the face of these difficulties. She appealed to his intelligence, urging him not to be upset, and not to follow his immediate impulses by revealing him to his wife and son, or by making premature vengeance on the pretenders. Such impulsive behavior would lead to failure. Ulysses and Athena then discussed how to bring about the demise of the unrestrained pretenders.

Athena transformed Ulysses into a beggar so that he could enter his own palace without risk, and see for himself the arrogance of the pretenders, and suffer vexation in silence while he waited for the opportune moment. We see here a similar process to that described in Ulysses' encounter with the Cyclops. In both cases, vengeance is preceeded and made possible by the self-denial of his own character. With the Cyclops, Ulysses was "no one," and in the present case he was a "beggar," a socially nonexistent entity.[6] Such identity confusion can produce a "surprise effect" that may make defeating the enemy easier. But the device may also be seen as a moment in the "annullment" of vengeance in its more elementary form. For the first time, vengeance, as an uncontrollable impulse, is temporarily denied. However, since vengeance is the essential reason for a strategic action, once this course of action is begun, it must be unswervingly carried through to its end. The regulation of vengeance itself is now "controllable" by the individual, and also becomes progressively structured into social organization. This means that vengeance, though old, has become "new."

Ulysses' waiting is now at an end. Penelope, who as a faithful wife, had tried in every way to restrain the pretenders,[7] proposed a competition to see who could draw Ulysses' bow and shoot an arrow through the rings of twelve axe heads. The winner would be her new husband. None of the pretenders was able to draw the bow. Ulysses took his turn, drew the bow easily, and his first arrow sailed straight through the twelve rings. His vengeance began with the killing of Antinous, the leader of the pretenders.

Ulysses eventually revealed himself, and began the battle against his enemies who now realized that they had no hope of escape. First, they tried to lay all the blame on the dead Antinous, but because of Ulysses' relentless onslaught, they had no choice but to defend themselves. Even though they outnumbered him, they were rapidly defeated by Ulysses, his son, and a few others, because Ulysses' sudden appearance had caught them totally off guard.

After clearing the field of his enemies, Ulysses reestablished himself in his home, but before he could be totally assured of victory, he had to convince Penelope that it was really he. She was soon convinced of this when he revealed facts to her that only she and Ulysses could have known.[8]

The need for the legitimation of the family relationship shows the presence of a definite patriarchal and monarchical order. Within this order, vengeance itself appears as a means to control and maintain that same order. We see the very important beginning of the transformation of vengeance into a sort of "judiridical procedure," even if still essentially a private justice.

In this regard, we may observe the executions of the traitor Melanthios and the slave girls who had been unfaithful.[9] The two are quite different. While Melanthios was executed by amputating his nose, ears, and genitals (which were then thrown to the dogs), the slave girls were simply hanged. The readers are spared the description of the crude particulars of the girls' execution. Instead, the tone of the description and the reaction of Ulysses to this last act of vengeance against the slave girls is similar to a modern news report about the implementation of capital punishment: a formal report purged of its emotive quality. In objective terms, it is "necessary" for the restoration of the equilibrium upset by their crimes.

The Odyssey concludes with the complete restoration of the patriarchal order. The intervention of Athena as "deus ex machina" in preventing the pretenders' allies from retaliating against Ulysses' vengeance stops the natural tendency for a long and bloody feud. We can see here the contrasting needs of the social order and that of reciprocity. The gods must still intervene in order to put a stop to the destructiveness of vengeance, because mankind cannot yet do this for itself.

The introduction of a "third (human) party," such as the Athenian Areopagus (well described in the trilogy of Aeschylus) is the next step in the progression of vengeance from the primitive to the "civilized."

Civilizing Vengeance: The Trial of Orestes

> Orestes is acquitted of blood guiltiness.
> —*The Eumenides* of Aeschylus.[10]

The Oresteian trilogy tells the story of the house of Atreus during the period following the Trojan war. Vengeance is the driving force of all action in these tragedies, but, as we shall see, the main thrust of the works is directed more towards a family tragedy, which is renewed with each generation. Thus, we are led to the discovery of general themes concerning interpersonal relationships that provide the context for a tentative definition of "justice."

According to legend, there was a conflict between the two brothers Atreus and Thyestes for the throne of the kingdom of Mycenae. Already hanging over these two brothers was a heavy burden of guilt for having murdered their younger brother Chrysippus. For this act, a curse was placed on them by their father Pelops. The relationship between the two brothers is the worst in all Greek mythology. Thyestes seduced his brother's wife, and Atreus, in retaliation, killed his brother's children and served them to their father, who unknowingly ate them. Thyestes placed a curse on Atreus and all his descendants, among whom were Agamemnon and Menelaus.

These two brothers married two sisters, Clytemnestra and Helen. The curse would lead, as described in the trilogy, to the vengeance of the only surviving child of Thyestes, Aegisthus, and to a chain of retaliations from every side, seemingly impossible to stop. Agamemnon, following in this tradition, sacrificed his daughter Iphigenia in order to mount his expedition against Troy, thus inviting the mortal hatred of his wife, Clytemnestra.

In the first three tragedies, *Agamemnon* returns to his home after his victory over the Trojans. There he is killed by his wife Clytemnestra who, during his absence, had become the lover of his cousin Aegisthus (Thyestes' son). They had united in order to perpetrate a common act of vengeance against the unfortunate Agamemnon.

In the second tragedy, *Choephori*, vengeance is wrought upon Agamemnon's son Orestes, who, with his sister Electra, had killed their mother and her lover Aegisthus in retaliation for the death of Agamemnon. For carrying out this "duty," Orestes is persecuted by the Furies.

The last tragedy, *The Eumenides*, proposes a solution to this endless cycle of familial murder. Orestes submits to the judgment of the goddess Athena, and to the "court of justice," the Aereopagus. In this trial, the Furies play the part of "public prosecutor," while Apollo who inspired Orestes to matricide, plays the part of "public defender." Once it was recognized that Orestes had gone through a period of "moral suffering" as a consequence of his act, his guilt is expiated, he is "acquitted of blood guiltiness" and set free.

The spiral of retaliation is, in this way, interrupted, and the way is paved for a new period in which vengeance is no longer automatic, but is subject to a "higher" social order. Aeschylus proposes a "judicial solution" to the problem of the relationship between vengeance and justice—the solution being the institution of the Areopagus. The archaic forces of vengeance are impersonated by the Furies whose main function is to punish crimes between relatives, and as well those of blasphemy, and offenses against guests. This function is clearly expressed in the tragedy.[11]

> No hope can rescue him
> A mother's blood once spilt
> None can restore again
>
> In payment for her blood
> In penance for her pain
> Down to the world of death
> Mark this: not only you
> But every mortal soul
> Whose pride has once transgressed
> The law of reverence due
> To parent, god or guest
> Shall pay sin's just inexorable toll.

They inexorably persecute every transgression of these principles, and during the tragedy it is shown that, according to the mechanical application of vengeance, it is practically impossible to put an end to an endless chain of killings.

A more civilized application of vengeance is represented by the god Apollo who promoted the "Delphic Code" as well as Olympic justice. Apollo speaks through the oracle at Delphi. As Vellacott pointed out:

Just as the Hebrew law of the Old Testament, "An eye for an eye, a tooth for a tooth" imposed an exact limit on the indiscriminate vengeance of primitive savagery, so the Delphic Code enjoined the taking of life for a life by the next of kin to a murdered man, and then offered to purify the avenger by ritual cleansing and so avoid further murders and an endless feud. Apollo instructed Orestes to kill his mother; an act which Orestes himself abhorred as deeply as anyone would since it is an offense against the tenderest of all natural affections.[12]

The figure of Clytemnestra is perhaps the most interesting character of the Trilogy. She is doubly outraged by Agamemnon, as wife and mother. Her drive for vengeance changes her from nurturer to destroyer. She assumes a kind of "male" character—"Clytemnestra, in whose woman's heart a man's will nurses hope."[13] In this ambivalence lies the originality of her character. As a female, she displays the characteristic submission of a woman of her time, but refusing this role, she demands a reciprocal solution, revealing her attempt to re-place the "tyrant-husband" by herself becoming the "king." These events show clearly the contradictions that inhere in the relationship between men and women within and without the immediate family, highlighting the forces of envy and "ressentiment." Obviously, most families do not solve their problems by killing each other, as did Clytemnestra. But we do see in this story the failure of Clytemnestra to sublimate the elementary sense of injustice that derives from the submissiveness required of the female. Aeschylus shows how a normal relationship between husband and wife can turn from a complementary relationship of dominance and submission to one of "reciprocity between equals," thus reproducing the mechanisms of father/tyrant and son/hero that we have described in chapter 1.

In assuming the male-father role, Clytemnestra not only denies herself as female (the adultery with Aegisthus appears to be simply her way of attaining absolute power), she also (in the style of the gods we described in chapter 1) banishes her son, and keeps her daughter Electra in a slave-like condition.

The antagonism among generations shows a high degree of repression at work. The tyrannical figure is, in this case, split in two: Agamemnon, and Clytemnestra who is openly persecutory. Thus, we can understand the profound ambivalence of Orestes' wish—forced to love and to hate, at the same time, the one object, his mother Clytemnestra. The figure of the good father is paradoxically represented by Agamemnon whose "guilt" is surely not of less magnitude than that of his wife.

In this web of passion and misdeeds embedded in the cycle of vengeance, Aeschylus poses a solution that coincides with a primitive concept of justice in a retributive sense. This solution requires a transformation of the old chthonic divinities, the vengeful Furies, into the kindly Eumenides, goddesses of the ciy after having lost their primordial characteristics.

The "Discovery" of Expiation

The most significant point about Aeschylus' solution is that for the first time the judgment about a private dispute, which would ordinarily have been settled by repeated retaliation and aggression, was placed before an external authority. The trial also produces the early recognition in Western culture of "moral suffering" as a means of atoning for a wrongful act. It marks the beginning of the idea of expiation, a central theme of many modern notions of vengeance that we call "retribution."

We see in the acquittal of Orestes through his expiation the clear direction of punishment towards the offender's person, instead of against the act. That is, we should remember that the primitive form of vengeance was directed against any aggressive act, regardless of the perpetrator's motives. Now, in contrast, there is more of an individualization of punishment against the guilty. This expresses an essential association between punishment and desert. Punishment now has two essential attributes: it always purports to be inflicted not only for a bad act, but also upon the guilty person or persons.

This recognition presupposes a relatively developed society, in which a there is a set number of rules or regulations. Thus begins the delineation of the condition of true punishment that only exists where some system of rights has been violated by one who shares in it. The recognition of moral suffering by an external authority as a way of making up for a crime, has the important social effect of stopping the cycle of vengeance once the offended party has accepted the moral suffering of the other (expiation) as sufficient restitution of the wrong. This makes possible the exchange of an offense for a *symbolic recognition* instead of exchanging it for an aggressive act of equal intensity.

As we can see, the concept of expiation shows two closely connected aspects, each with its unique meaning. On the one hand, the moral suffering is accepted from the point of view of the offended person as a payment of the wrong, which in a certain way is a "debt" to the offended person himself (and to a certain extent the social body which identifies itself with the position of the offended person).[14] On the other hand, the same moral suffering, for instance in the Christian conception, considered from the point of view of the expiator, may be seen as a means to moral cleanliness by undergoing contrition. These two aspects of the concept of expiation recall the contradiction in the coexistence of the two models of reciprocity (according to who has requested the expiation through retribution) and obedience (through which one can reach salvation).

While reciprocity suggests the maximum point of evolution of classic culture, obedience becomes more and more valued in Christian culture. The Divine Comedy of Dante, in its evolution from vengeance (Inferno as expiation without any change of salvation), through obedience (Purgatory), to forgiveness (Paradise) displays with great mastery this second and perhaps contradictory nature of the idea of expiation.

Notes

1. Homer, *The Odyssey*, trans. W. H. D. Rouse (New York: Mentor, 1937), Book xx, p. 226.

2. Ibid., Book v, p. 75.

3. Dante visits a similar punishment on the hoarders and spendthrifts in the *Inferno*.

4. A similar approach to the Ulysses character in terms of the enlightenment spirit, is expounded by Horkheimer and Adorno. See M. Horkheimer and T. W. Adorno, *The Dialectic of the Enlightenment*, trans. J. Cumming (New York: Continuum, 1972), pp. 43–80.

5. Ibid., p. 106.

6. This device can also be seen as a means of presenting the self in functional terms, so as to fulfill a plan of action. See E. Goffman, *The Presentation of Self in Everyday Life* (N.Y.: Doubleday), 1959.

7. Penelope represents one of the first clearly defined female characters in classical literature. She is the prototype of the "wife" in a patriarchical society. The legend attributes to her the characteristic of patience. She had tricked the pretenders by weaving her cloth during the day, and undoing it

at night, claiming that she could not decide whether to get married again until the cloth was finished.

8. She asks him to move his bed, but he says that he cannot. Indeed this is so, since he had made his bed in a tree, and the tree could not be moved.

9. Adorno and Horkheimer, *Dialectic*, p. 79.

10. Aeschylus, *The Eumenides*, trans. P. Vellacott (London: Penguin, 1956), sc.. II, p. 173.

11. Ibid., sc. II, pp. 156–57.

12. Ibid., Introduction, pp. 17–18.

13. Ibid., Agamemnon, p. 41.

14. For a more detailed discussion of this view, see W. Moberly, in R. J. Gerber and P. D. McAnany, eds., *Contemporary Punishment* (Notre Dame: University of Notre Dame Press, 1972), p. 73.

4

Vengeance and the Sacred: Dante's Inferno

Thou bid'st me to renew a grief so desperate that the thought alone
Before I voice it, cracks my heart in two.
Yet, if indeed my words, like seedlings sown,
Shall fruit, to shame this traitor whom I tear,
Then shalt thou see me speak and weep in one.
—Dante Alighierei, Hell[1]

IN THE DEEPEST RECESSES OF HELL, two traitors suffer the eternal punishment of being frozen up to their necks in the icy lake Cocytus. While one of the two lies still and silent, the other, driven by an insatiable hunger, continues to devour his skull.

Dante is confronted with this powerful scene as he comes to the end of his journey through the City of Desolation. It is one of the most graphic scenes in all of Dante's works. The sinner, a traitor who is intent on devouring the skull of his victim, momentarily turns from his horrid feast, so that he can tell his story. The memory of the events that led to his death gives him much grief. However, he seizes the opportunity to heap blame on the other soul, thereby adding to his revenge, even in Hell.

The traitor is Count Ugolino who lived in Pisa in the latter half of the thirteenth century, and his victim is the Archbishop Roger. Ugolino, a Ghibelline, betrayed his family and his political faction to their mortal enemy, the Guelfs.[2] The plot was discovered and he was exiled, but after a short time, political fortunes changes, and he was able to return to Pisa under the protection of the Guelfs. He soon obtained an important public position. But, in 1288, Ugolino's former Ghibelline companions, led by Archbishop Roger (who had been Ugolino's master and friend), struck back by seizing Ugolino and putting him to death.

The Count continues the dialogue with Dante. He points out that, although Dante has probably heard of his story, he may not know the particulars of his death:

> How bitter cruel my death was; hear, and then
> If he has done me injury, judge thou.[3]

Ugolino was locked in a tower with two sons and two nephews who were very young. After some months, the door to the prison was nailed shut, and Ugolino immediately understood that his death had been decided: it would be by starvation. Trying to restrain himself, and show strength to the boys, he did not speak for the entire day. But when the dawn of the next day came, the tragedy slowly unfolded as Ugolino realized that the boys now also clearly understood their fate. At this point, he temporarily lost control, biting his knuckles bloody, thus presaging the vengeance in Hell when he would consume the hated archbishop Roger.

To Dante's horror, Ugolino describes his death and that of his sons and nephews:

> As thou doest see me here, I saw him die
> And one by one the other three dies too,
> From the fifth day to the sixth. Already I
> Was Blind; I took to fumbling them over; two
> Long days I groped there, calling on the dead
> Then famine did what sorrow could not do.[4]

The image of The Count, almost blind, groping his way around the corpses, is the prelude to the dramatic conclusion of the story.

Ugolino probably ate the corpses of his sons, as we can see from his last words—"famine did what sorrow could not do." This suggestion is confirmed by other historical sources.[5] In reporting this dark story of treason and homicide, Ugolino is presented as the strongest figure of vengeance in the entire *Hell*. His hatred is absolute, and is only momentarily appeased by the atrocious retaliation that he is authorized to inflict on the archbishop. He almost does not notice Dante's presence. His only wish is to damage his enemy in any way.

The Scale of Justice

In this story, Dante's fantasy points out the progressively destructive dynamic of the cycle of vengeance. Ugolino first betrays his family and his political party, and Roger repays Ugolino for his wrong, but adds to it the death of Ugolino's sons. The sons' deaths are obviously a part of Roger's vindictive design. The Count's punishment, which is in itself terrible, is made more bitter by the sense of guilt of Ugolino who involuntarily causes the deaths of his most beloved sons. Part of the same vengeance is, moreover, the design to drive Ugolino crazy, and to force him, against his will, to eat the flesh of his sons, to reduce him to the lowest depths of self-degradation.

The *scale* of justice is quite remarkably shaken free of any limits to moderation in this episode because four innocent children (except for the fact that they were Ugolino's relatives)[6] were killed simply in order to return vengeance in tremendous force. The norm of reciprocity is therefore perverted into one in which it is necessary to return more than was received. The fact that innocent lives were taken in order to achieve this end seems to be beside the point—and indeed seems only minimally important to Ugolino in so far as it contributed to *his* suffering.[7] The essentially coercive nature of vengeance is thus enhanced, and as we shall see, becomes the main point of punishment throughout Dante's trilogy.[8] However, in order to match Roger's dreadful crime, Ugolino has the final "retribution"—devouring Roger's skull for eternity.

This story clearly demonstrates the principle of reflection in vengeful punishment. Ugolino is punished for his treason and for his excessive *thirst* for power with death by *starvation*. His vengeance also reflects the crime of the archbishop—the death of Ugolino and its cannibalistic aspect, since in Hell, Roger is literally eaten by the Count. It is no coincidence that the part of the body eaten by Ugolino, to satisfy his insatiable hunger, is the head of his enemy. From that brain was born the idea of vengeance against him.

In *Hell* the roles are inverted. The vengeance of Roger

against Ugolino is turned into eternal punishment. The traitor Ugolino is himself betrayed; and the betrayed Roger becomes the real traitor of the story.

In this progressive escalation of vengeance, the real vengeful principle, and one much more powerful than both the characters of Ugolino and Roger, is the Divine Will that, while it inflicts an endless punishment on both sinners, also uses the same Ugolino in order to inflict an additional punishment on Roger. Ugolino, who is forced to repeat the punishment compulsively, is only temporarily appeased in his thirst for vengeance; we cannot say that he is truly fulfilled in his vengeance. Furthermore, the constant contact and proximity with the sources of his grief and hate, not only do not allow him relief, but are the source of even more grief.

In this way, vengeance is clearly part of the punishment that God has decided to inflict upon him. However, in this respect, we must say that Dante's God is not an "even-handed" God. The punishments, while carefully matched in classic vengeful fashion, seem especially coercive. This is because they must serve a *moral* purpose: they must, while they are punishments, also perform the task of establishing a meaningful link between punishment and guilt. Dante achieves this through the idea of expiation.

Vengeance as Expiation

The concept of expiation as moral suffering appears in the Greek tragedies, but in Dante, it is now completely systematized. Expiation is used to connect guilt with punishment in two distinct ways.

First, in *Hell*, the main concern is still with "payment" for the sin in the form of eternal contrition without any hope, within a clearly vengeful framework. This book represents the first stage of the soul's journey to salvation, which, according to Dante, consists in the transformation from absolute sin to absolute purity—reached only in the highest echelons of Paradise in front of the Divinity. One begins this cleansing journey in the deepest abyss of evil which, in *Hell*, is represented as eternal and incurable.

Second, in *Purgatory*, a curative function is clearly expressed, and suffering is given a different purpose apart from simple payment for a wrongful deed. Here, hope is introduced through the possibility of forgiveness, and temporal limits are set to the punishments. The souls are prepared for entrance into Paradise. This concept constitutes the major innovation in the Judeo-Christian tradition after the Old Testament. The concept of moral suffering, as a means of payment for a wrong, follows after the talion principle, via the Delphic code, finally to find expression in the concepts of contrition and expiation in the Roman Catholic liturgy.

Once the condition of contrition is recognized as a means of symbolic payment, it has the effect of helping to break the cycle of vengeance. Previously, the only regulation was through *lex talionis*, which "ordered," from each side, retaliations equal in both quantity and quality.

We also see that our two models of reciprocity and obedience are intertwined: from the point of view of the expiator, it must be obedience that is of central concern, but from the point of view of the punisher, the quest for vengeance, the correct application of an appropriate and matching punishment is of importance. As Newman has clearly pointed out, it is necessary to develop a distinction between the secular and religious versions of the retributive conception.[9] It is clear that the latter version tends to display an evolution, the end of which produces the contrary of vengeance—forgiveness.

This change is obtained through the idea of expiation:

> The religious version of retribution requires basically two things: the crime must be resolved through its punishment, and the punishment must involve long term suffering. . . . The religious retributivists naturally take the word "guilt" in its moral sense, which is to say that the offender has a "guilty" mind, that only by a series of ritual purgative functions can this guilt be assuaged. Therefore one must not only fit the punishment to the crime, but one must fit the punishment to the criminal's guilty mind.[10]

We can see that along the road from *Hell*, through Purgatory to Paradise, the concern is focused more and more on the expiation of the guilty mind. According to this conception, Dante does not establish one simple classification of "crime," but more accurately, establishes categories of "sins," which are evil dispositions of the soul. Crime derives from these dispositions. This is why gluttons and the murderers are punished equally, forever, although in different degrees of intensity.

Newman defines the consequences of the religious conception of retribution.

Although, strictly speaking, according to the old retributivists one should only match a single crime with a single punishment, it is clear from the religious view of retribution that one must match the despicable criminal sins with the punishments. In other words, one must go beyond the particular offense to the soul of the offender. By this model one is justified in matching the punishment to the criminal's entire person.[11]

It must be clear, Newman observes, that according to Dante, the punishment that resolves the crime by its symbolic reflection, is undoubtedly a punishment that intentionally and deliberately inflicts pain.[12] This differs substantially from this century's basic ideology of correctional penology that seeks to "treat" the offender, and ostensibly avoid the infliction of pain.[13] It does, however, allow the suffering of innocent family members to continue, in the same tradition as occurred with Ugolino.

The Symbolic Transformation of Vengenace

In *Hell*, contrition is eternal. It is written on the gates of Hell:

> Through me the road to the city of desolation,
> Through me the road to sorrows diuturnal,
> Through me the road among the lost creation.
> Justice moved my great maker.[14]

Therefore, we must conclude that this justice has, as its fundamental element, the fact of vengeful action. First of all, in *Hell*, that which was taken is given back as an eternal punishment. Then, what is given back is by definition more of what had been taken. This is because the Infernal punishments are identical in quality to the offenses, but are not identical in quantity, since they are endless. The "repayment" is certainly not of the concrete kind in the sense that it is a "life for a life" as, for example, with Achilles and Hector, or Clytemnestra and Agamemnon. There is the additional intent to add a *moral* reflection or lesson concerning the evil of the crime. The application of the punishment in the form of a symbolic reflection of the offense is the *raison d'être* of Hell. All crimes are beautifully matched by their punishments.[15] This reflective conception of punishment (known as the law of "contrapasso") is an evolution of the talion principle into a more abstract form. In this sense, it is part of the civilizing process of vengeance.[16]

Dante has thus developed the talion principle into a highly sophisticated form that clearly reflects the moral error of each offense in each punishment. For instance, according to Dante's classification, the Lustful are continuously thrust about by a terrible storm which symbolizes the turbulence of their desires on earth.

> The blast of hell that never rests from whirling
> Harries the spirits along in the sweep of its swath
> And vexes them, for ever beating and hurling.[17]

Violent offenders must lie submersed in a river of boiling blood, a reminder of the blood that they have spilled on earth. They suffer violence themselves because they are the eternal targets of the Centaurs' arrows.[18] In the Infernal bowges, the hypocrites are forced to walk eternally under the weight of leaden capes that look, on the outside, as though they are golden. We see here the clear allusion to the double image that these hypocrites made of their lives.

The symbolic reflection of the punishment portrays both the quality of the sin and its gravity; and the more serious the sin, the deeper in Hell one finds the soul. We see here a very important innovation—the introduction of an imposed order into vengeance.

Giving Order to Vengeance

The Infernal judge, Minos, whom Dante meets immediately on entering the eternal prison, takes charge of the distribution of souls throughout Hell. This scene is described by Dante:

> There in the threshold, horrible and girning,
> Grim Minos sits, holding his ghastly session,
> And, as he girds him, sentencing and spurning;
> For when the ill soul faces him, confession
> Pours out of him till nothing's left to tell
> Whereon that connoisseur of all transgression
> Assigns it to its proper place in Hell,
> As many grades as he would have it fall,
> So oft he belts him round with his own tail.[19]

Although eternity is common to all forms of punishment in *Hell*, there is a classification that provides for different degrees of gravity for the guilty. Dante's classification follows the established order of the scholastic philosophers, derived essentially from the classical Greeks, particularly from Aristotle's *Ethics*. This is clearly said in BOOK XI, where Dante explains the principle of the distribution of the Souls.[20]

According to this conception, the original source of all sins is due to three "dispositions of the soul" (the three dispositions that Heaven does not want), namely, incontinence, force, and fraud. The duty of the Infernal machine is to properly punish the sins and the particular crimes that derive from the sins, as well as the dispositions that cause them.

Incontinence, force, and fraud, correspond roughly to the three zones that divide *Hell* into progressive degrees of gravity. The rationale for this classification is provided by Dante thus: the incontinent and the violent are not unlike animals. They are "not human" in some way, because the source of their guilt is the impossibility to restrain or control their impulses. They are therefore less responsible than the fraudulent who display a voluntary disposition by using the exclusively human faculty of reason.

Thus, the fraudulent are punished more than any other category of sinners. Among these, traitors are presented as the worst or most evil category of the fraudulent (among whom may be counted the panderers and seducers, thieves, sowers of discord, falsifiers, sorcerers, and simoniacs). They are the worst, because they betray the trust of others—they are traitors to family, country, and guests. Dante reserves for these worst sinners the deepest recess of Hell that, perhaps unexpectedly, is no blazing inferno, but the frozen lake of Cocytus. Such was the appropriate place for Ugolino, the arch-traitor who *coldly* and calculatedly betrayed the trust of his friends.

Treason: The Worst Offense

Notwithstanding Dante's "rational" arrangement of the severity of punishment according to the progressive use of human faculties, we can argue that, in reality, treason is always seen as the most serious crime, because it is the one crime that recalls the original crime of rebellion against the principal of authority. We will also see, in later chapters, that this is a main theme in the legends of the Lone Avengers, Jesse James, and in feuding societies. If the legendary heroes are killed at all, it is invariably because they are betrayed by a trusted relative or friend. As Freud said:

> In the Christian myth, the original sin is undoubtedly an offense
> against the father/god. Now, if Christ set men free from the burden of
> original sin, sacrificing his own life, it forces us to conclude that this
> original offense was a murder. According to the talion principle that is
> deeply rooted in human sensibility, a murder could be expiated only
> with the sacrifice of another life. The sacrifice of himself takes us back
> to a homicide . . . in this way mankind confesses in a more open way,
> in the Christian doctrine, the guilty action committed literally in the
> night of the ages.[21]

So, the original crime, having issued from the elementary
sense of injustice, provoked a retaliation from Authority that
equated rebellion with treason. As we saw earlier, the solution
was also the repression of the wish to rebel, and this repression would also condemn rebellion as the most serious crime
of all. If the original crime was that of rebellion, it is understandable that Dante's scheme would punish rebellion more
than anything else, since it is a rebellion against a divine
Authority.

We can now argue that the Trilogy provides us with a
scheme of evolution from vengeance to forgiveness, and as
well, a way out of the cultural nexus of man—the guilt of the
primal crime. If the death of Christ was necessary to pay for
the offense against the divinity, now it is possible to let
vengeance go, and instead achieve forgiveness through expiation and obedience. By reaching a condition of complete
obedience, one can achieve an identification with the principal of authority itself—God.

Here it is possible to see the process of repression reaching
its greatest heights of identification with an absolute principle
of authority, but at the cost of total obedience, and riding
rough-shod over the principle of reciprocity. According to the
Freudian interpretation of the birth of social order, one of the
first effects of repression was the creation of the social bond on
the basis of reciprocity. This bond was that which grew out of
the agreement among the band of brothers not to continue
individual acts of violence after they had first acted together to
kill the father.

Paradoxically, the first crime of treason was also the main
threat to the maintenance of the social order. This is why, from
the very beginning, society has always punished treason more
than murder.

Summary

Through Dante's genius, we are provided with a glimpse of the role of vengeance within a highly complex and developed system of punishment and guilt that prevailed towards the end of the Middle Ages. Typical of this scheme was a high degree of ritualization, and a careful construction of punishments that performed a specific function. The development of ritual in vengeance, and in punishment in general, constitutes a basic trait of vengeance, which becomes more and more important with the development of repression as society becomes more complex.

At the same time, the problem of justifying vengeance has been addressed. As we have observed, this problem is inextricably related to the development of ritual. What once were pure acts of aggression were slowly transformed into ritualistic acts (perhaps the totemic feast was the first of these), or at least acts that required attempts by the actors to justify them. Avenging acts were, and are, ritualistic. Indeed, the special ways of killing others, dictated in a number of feuding subcultures, are typical examples of such ritualism.[22] The ways of killing that we have described in the Oresteian tragedy were certainly full of ritual.

Dante's *Hell* is one of the most complete manifestations of a vengeful system. But, as we have observed, the concept of vengeance in the Christian liturgy is part of a process that also denies the premise of vengeance itself. The development of the systematic and ritualized process of punishment and its justification reveals that obedience is the real objective and the reason for the journey of the soul through the three realms of the other world.

Through these visions of sins and their punishments, the man of the Middle Ages reached his complete maturity, and the Church provided the most powerful ideological justification for domination. In the following centuries, man, lacking this supportive ideology, has had to face again and again his never-forgotten wish for reciprocity. Without any external aid for instance, Prince Hamlet was not able simply to observe, as was Dante, the suffering of *Hell*, as a mere stage in his journey towards Paradise. Rather, Hamlet was forced to consider guilt and punishment as a problem that needed an earthly solution, which meant that he had to assume full responsibility for his acts.

Notes

1. Dante Alighieri, *The Divine Comedy: Hell* (London: Penguin, 1979), XXXIII, vv. 4–9, p. 278.

2. This was the period in Tuscany when city states dominated, and many political factions vied with each other for influence. The Guelfs and the Ghibellines were two of the dominant factions of the period. Political power constantly fluctuated back and forth between them.

3. *Hell*, XXXIII, vv. 20–21, p. 278.

4. Ibid., XXXIII, vv. 70–75, p. 280.

5. "The thesis that Ugolino would have eaten the corpses of his sons is attested to in a chronicle of the thirteenth century edited by Villari, *I Primi due secoli della storia di Firenze* p. 256, where it is written that it was found in the prison that one had eaten of the flesh of the others . . . the bestial fury of Ugolino against Roger could not be justified otherwise. It is the terrible eternal vengeance of the Count, who in the delirium preceeding his death, almost blind in his mind as well as his eyes, gropes like a wild beast over the corpses of his sons, eating their flesh." See Dante Alighieri, *La Divina Commedia* (Roma: Editori Riuniti, 1980), p. 440, our translation.

6. We will see in chapters 6 through 9 that this is not so unusual a circumstance. In feuding societies, family ties are the only meaningful social relationship recognized, so that an offense against the member of one family is considered an offense against the entire family; a vengeful act is therefore logically acceptable against any relative of an offender.

7. That is, the concern is not focused on the children who died simply so that Ugolino's suffering might be more severe.

8. Of course, treason is a very serious crime, for reasons noted later in this chapter. One might argue, therefore, that the loss of four innocent lives plus the life of the guilty is a reasonable "matching" of the crime with its punishment. The logical basis of this match, however, does not seem readily apparent. For a discussion of this problem, see Graeme Newman, *Just and Painful: A Case for the Corporal Punishment of Criminals* (New York: Macmillan, 1983) passim.

10. Newman, *Just and Painful*, pp. 64–65.

11. Ibid., p. 68.

12. Furthermore, as we noted above, the intention to inflict pain is so singleminded that the infliction of suffering on innocents (e.g., Ugolino's relatives) is considered reasonable, especially if it enhances the suffering of the offender. Today, this ethic continues in our use of prison as a punishment, regardless of the suffering it causes the offender's innocent family members. Ibid.

13. Ibid., p. 67.

14. *Hell*, IV, vv. 1–4, p. 85.

15. Newman, *Just and Painful*, p. 64.

16. That is, on the presumption made by some students of western

culture, that the essential feature of the civilizing process, or a civilized society is the capacity to think abstractly. See S. Garn, ed., *Culture and the Direction of Evolution* Detroit (Wayne State University Press, 1964).

17. *Hell*, v, vv. 31–33, p. 98.

18. A centaur is a mythical beast, half man and half horse, violent and rapacious.

19. *Hell*, v, vv. 4–12, p. 97.

20. *Hell*, II, pp. 134–137.

21. S. Freud, *Totem and Taboo*, trans. J. Strachey (New York: Norton, 1950) p. 102.

22. See, for example, chapters 7 through 9, especially in regard to the ritual ways in which victims were killed.

5

Vengeance and Responsibility: Hamlet's Procrastination

Hamlet: Speak, I am bound to hear
Ghost: So art thou to revenge[1]

THE STORY OF THE Prince of Denmark and his procrastination wonderfully illustrates the need for vengeance and, at the same time, the impossibility of its ultimate fulfilment.

Hamlet's duty is to avenge his father who was killed by the treacherous act of his uncle, who in turn replaced Hamlet's father as king and husband of his mother. This duty is not implemented until the end of the last scene when the hero himself is about to die.

At the beginning of the play, Hamlet looks anxious and depressed, and in the first soliloquy, contemplates suicide.

Or that the Everlasting had not
fixed his canon 'gainst self-slaughter . . .[2]

Hamlet strongly associates this idea of suicide with the wedding of his mother to his uncle, which had followed shortly after the death of his father.

Hamlet's hatred for his stepfather Claudius and his indignation at his mother's conduct seem to be out of proportion to the gravity of their actions. His mother's marriage may have been hasty, but it was, at the time, acceptable. This leads us to conclude that the source of Hamlet's resentment was deep, and probably unconscious.

The Internalization of Vengeance

In the dialogue between Hamlet and his father's ghost, we see Hamlet's psychic conflict. The ghost reveals that Claudius is the murderer, and asks Hamlet to carry out his duty to avenge this crime, a request that the Prince himself had forseen ("Oh my prophetic soul, my uncle"). Implicitly, the ghost poses the problem of how to bear the responsibility of carrying out and not carrying out vengeance at the same time. "This Time is out of joint," says Hamlet, "O curse spite, that ever I was born to set it right."

Following this scene, Hamlet's behavior is somber and inconsistent. But the one most concerned is the uncle-murderer, who decides, for the sake of precaution, to send Hamlet away. In the drama that follows, Hamlet shows his typical character traits—a high degree of ambivalence towards females, severe hostility towards the males, and deep indecisiveness—or more in this case, the inability to "do his duty."

An example of his ambivalence toward women is his relationship with Ophelia, daughter of Polonius (first adviser to the king Claudius). During the dialogue with the young girl, Hamlet indulges in self blame:

> I am myself indifferent honest, but
> Yet I could accuse me of such things, that
> It were better my mother had not born me.[3]

There are contradictory statements of acceptance and rejection: "I did love you once . . . I loved you not"[4] Hamlet's confusion, the killing of the girl's father, and the terrible accusations Hamlet makes against her, lead Ophelia to madness and a suicide. We may note that while the murder of Polonius was carried out with indifference, Hamlet was unable to take advantage of the situation in which it would have been easy to kill his stepfather (his uncle). It is most significant that the uncle, in the course of his monologue, recognizes his own guilt:

> O my offense is rank,
> it smells to Heaven; It hath the primal eldest
> curse upon't, a brother's murder.[5]

This indecision underlies the entire tragedy. The father's ghost itself is almost forced to appear a final time to remind the Prince what has to be done:

> Do not forget;
> this visitation is but to whet
> thy most blunted purpose.[6]

Hamlet is tormented, accusing himself of weakness, and this is well expressed in the fourth act:

> How all occasion do inform against me
> And spur my dull revenge!
> . . . A thought which quartered hath but
> One part of wisdom, and ever three parts
> Coward—I do not know why I live to say
> This thing's to do . . . How stand I then, that have a
> Father killed, a mother stained, excitements of
> My reason and my blood, and let all sleep . . .
> O from this time forth, my thoughts be bloody
> Or be nothing worth . . .[7]

These words, better than any explanation, express the presence of a tremendous responsibility, seemingly impossible to bear. They express Hamlet's main problem: why is it impossible to carry out vengeance in the name of justice? We saw in chapter 3 that the Tragedies were unable to give a clear answer to this question, especially in the trial of Orestes. If gods could not answer it, perhaps we should not expect a confident solution from a very human Hamlet.

With his father Polonius and his sister Ophelia both dead as a result of Hamlet's "madness," Laertes returns from France with the express purpose of making revenge against Hamlet. Although their duty is similar, the will of Laertes is much stronger and he easily becomes a tool of Claudius, who is well aware of the risk presented by Hamlet.

Claudius arranges a duel that is made to appear harmless (Laertes' sword is supposed to be blunted, but is not—and it is coated with poison as well). And as if this were not enough, one of the cups of wine that is used to toast the winner is also poisoned. Hamlet's death is supposed to appear as an accident, but things do not go as planned.

First, the Queen drinks from the poisoned cup intended for Hamlet. Next, during the duel, the two combatants exchange swords so that they both are mortally wounded. At this point, Laertes reveals to Hamlet his stepfather's last intrigue. Claudius has caused the death of the Queen, and Hamlet knows that he too will soon die. By beating his stepfather to death, Hamlet at last fulfills his duty of vengeance.

The delay in fulfilling vengeance appears to be the least explicable in the entire drama. The Prince tends to substitute imagination or reflection for real action. The reason for this substitution of thought for action is not clear to Hamlet himself, and this is consistent with the impression of darkness and instability that his character makes on the audience. He is also prone to fits of doubt, suggesting a conflict between contradictory needs, only some of which are conscious.[8]

If we then hypothesize that at the bottom of Hamlet's attitude is a resistance to fulfilling the duty that he consciously wants to fulfill, this leads us to say that one part of his personality does not accept, indeed refuses, the same wish.

Vengeance: An Ambivalent Identification

By recognizing this profound ambivalence, we are able to decode the behavior of the Prince and, in addition, suggest an explanation for the theatrical and literary success of this character, which has survived so many interpretations over time. We can understand the perennial fascination that Hamlet holds for his audiences. This phenomenon cannot take place, we suggest, without an identification between the audience and the contradictory forces that constitute Hamlet's character. This is even more likely to occur if these forces lie in the unconscious. For this identification to be effective, it must have as its source certain collective psychological processes that have themes of general, or universal meaning. In other words, the conflict must be about something relatively constant from generation to generation.

In the story of Hamlet, we are able to recognize the essential elements of the original conflict: the elementary sense of injustice (caused by the usurpation of his father by Claudius), and the subsequent repression of the two fundamental drives that threaten the development of social order—namely, the hatred for the father, and the attraction to the mother.

Thus, the new marriage of the Queen to the brother of the dead husband appears to have reactivated these two repressed drives in Hamlet's psyche. The degree of intensity of these drives must have been very high and "unresolved," as psychoanalysts would say.

Vengeance and the Sense of Guilt

The process of repression has hidden more and more the real
nature of Hamlet's ambivalence, which lies at the bottom of
his inability to identify with the central figure of the conflict.
Following the talk with his father's ghost, it would seem
logical that Hamlet should embark on a realistic plan of
action. Instead, his every act from this point on is inhibited,
never reaching fulfillment. At the same time, he continually
asks himself why he does not do what seems to him obvious
what he should do.

The presence of these unresolved conflicts—the aggressive
feeling against the authority figure (the original father); the
attraction to the mother; and the power of the ego that must
control these forces, keeping them from consciousness, provide a plausible explanation for Hamlet's sense of guilt and
subsequent procrastination. In the early phase of this process,
according to this interpretation, Hamlet probably should have
rejected both these impulses, and "lived with" them in a
condition of relative equilibrium. But as we know, later when
his father is dead, his sense of guilt becomes stronger because
he probably felt himself responsible for what he had "in
reality" wished (that is, the death of his father). In the first
stage of this process, two paternal figures are created in
Hamlet's mind, one of them made by the memory of the good
father, and the other by the evil stepfather/uncle.

We can say that both these figures are the product of the
suppression of the "unconfessible" wish of Hamlet, and both
figures fulfill basic psychological needs. Through the creation
of the first, the sense of guilt is appeased, because the father,
originally hated, is now transformed into a benevolent figure.
Through the creation of the second, the same sense of guilt is
neutralized through the displacement of hostility onto an
external figure.

On this point, it is worth noting that the repressed drives
are still unresolved in the sense that the repression itself did
not lead, because of the great force of the drives, to a sufficient
identification with a paternal figure. In other words, the process that normally determines the acceptance of the paternal
role (the autonomy of adulthood), which is characteristic of a
mature identity, did not occur. This is because we have seen

that Hamlet's problem is also one of an incomplete realization of his own identity.

Hamlet's difficulty in exercising the normal mechanisms of repression results in his being unable to maintain the normal level of ambivalence that accompanies everyone's life in the relationship with their parents. The difficulty is obviously exacerbated by the fact that the beloved father is not dead from "natural causes," but is actually the victim of a terrible crime. At this point, the precarious equilibrium between drives and repression is definitely altered. The creation of the two paternal figures also adds the function of controlling the strong sense of guilt derived from the original conflict. It is not sufficient any longer to contain the force of the drives so that the "bad" father, actually realizing the repressed fantasies of Hamlet, comes too close to the consciousness of the hero. This forces the repression to an even stronger intensity, which leads to an even stronger sense of guilt.

It is now very clear why Claudius, in committing a most odious crime against his brother, impersonates that part of Hamlet's personality that really wants to commit the crime. Above all, it is clear that the conscious part of the same personality rejected this wish, and instead, multiplied the hate against the "alter ego," proceeding toward its destruction.

Consequently, the unique problem of vengeance that faces Hamlet (that is, unconscious vengeance against the hated father) is more exactly a vengeance against himself—that part of him that is represented by the stepfather.

Hamlet's hopeless contradiction makes only one solution possible—suicide. And so at the end of the play, the protagonist realizes the impossible compromise between fulfilment of vengeance, assumption of his responsibilities, and satisfaction of his need for identification with the murderer of his father.

The impossibility of reaching his objective makes clear the contradiction inherent in the idea of vengeance when it is taken to the extreme.

Vengeance and Responsibility

We saw earlier in this book that vengeance was originally a reaction to the elementary sense of injustice, beginning in the eternal conflict between father and son, always remaining as an underlying need, but forced more and more to express itself in a socially "acceptable" form. This means that it has been subjected, for reasons of survival, to a process of repression. We find in this process tension between the two models— reciprocity and obedience, the interplay of which affects the same dynamic of social order. The repressive process and subsequent sense of guilt introduce the problem of "responsibility" for vengeance. In Hamlet, this "responsibility" is absolute in that the sense of guilt leads to the death of the hero. Only when this sense of guilt is appeased (that is, when Hamlet faces death) can he be free to do his duty.

The destiny of Hamlet is decided by his character, considering that the terms of the contradiction are inside himself, and not external as was the case in the time of the Greeks. As Jones says:

> In exhibiting the struggle between man and fate, Shakespeare achieved the very essence of the Greek conception of tragedy, but he went beyond this and showed that the essence of Man's fate is inherent in his own soul.[9]

In the case of Hamlet, however, we can see a great difference with respect to the development and resolution of the conflict compared to the classical era—due, as Freud said, "to the century old progression of repression in the emotional life of humanity."[10] For the Greeks, responsibility was external—the "will of the gods." But now we see a definite shift to internalize responsibility. The procrastination and the weighing of the pros and cons of reaping revenge, instead of being argued about among the gods as in the Oresteian Trilogy, are argued out in Hamlet's mind. These are classic tales demonstrating the ambivalence between father and son, punisher and expiator, still valid today (e.g. the movie Star Wars in which Luke Skywalker confronts his tyrant father Darth Vader) as they were thousands of years ago.

Furthermore, we see in these modern romances (though they are in fact tragedies) how man has learned to anticipate, in an acute way, the guilt that will be felt after the act of vengeance. Indeed, the anticipation is so keen that the guilt is felt even before the act—in fact, according to psychoanalysts, it is felt merely as a result of wishing for vengeance, even if the wish is never carried out.

This is what we mean by individual responsibility for

vengeance. It is essentially a guilt feeling, possibly felt more intensely than the original sense of injustice that has so driven man to seek vengeance in the first place. Such responsibility is often too much for ordinary mortals to bear. The Greeks understood this, and were able to transfer the responsibility to the gods. But now, demystified man can no longer take this easy way out. This is why vengeance today is so often carried out collectively. The responsibility can be more easily born (avoided may be more accurate) if others join in the vengeful act. The paradox here is that, as we have shown in chapter 1, collective action for reasons of vengeance is very primitive, and accounts, according to many of the Greek myths, for the basic, protypical acts of vengeance against authority.

Summary

We have shown that, with the emergence of psychological man, vengeance has been internalized, exhibiting itself as moral conflict. But this stage in the "development" of vengeance, concerned as it is with the typically modern preoccupation with "identity," is "progress" based on shaky foundations. It necessarily leads back to an earlier effective way of handling vengeance when individual responsibility was too much to bear and there was no concept of individual responsibility; it leads back to collective action.

We are able, using this model, to explain many diverse phenomena, such as the vengefulness of juvenile gangs, feuds, and even wars. We begin to see that collective vengeance is much more difficult to control because it is potentially so violent, and this takes us full circle, face to face with the raw element of vengeance—power.

Notes

1. *Hamlet*, Act I, sc. 5.
2. Op. cit., Act II, sc. 2.
3. Op. cit., Act III, sc. i.
4. Op. cit., Act III, sc. i.
5. Op. cit., Act III, sc. iii.
6. Op. cit., Act III, sc. iv.
7. Op. cit., Act IV, sc. iv.
8. As Jones clearly pointed out, "In recognizing Hamlet's non-con-

sciousness of the cause of his repugnance to his task, we are nearing the core of the mystery." E. Jones, *Hamlet and Oedipus* (Garden City, N.Y.: Doubleday, 1954) p. 55.

9. Ibid.

10. Freud, *Totem and Taboo*.

6

Cultures of Vengeance

And slay not the life which Allah hath forbidden save with right. Whoso is slain wrongfully, we have given power unto his heir, but let him not commit excess in slaying!

—*Koran*, XVII, 33

Feud: A Delicate Balance

THE OXFORD ENGLISH DICTIONARY defines a feud as "a state of perpetual hostility between two families, tribes, or individuals, marked by murderous assaults in revenge for some previous insult or injury." The feud is one of the most ancient procedures for "doing justice." It is also one of the most ancient forms of violence, particularly "organized violence." The "pure feud" is usually taken to be that in which collective responsibility predominates: if an individual commits a wrongful act, his whole tribe, family or clan is held responsible for the act, as is the victim's tribe or family held responsible for avenging the act.

In the earlier chapters of this book, we referred to collective rebellion as the most primitive form of vengeance, and possibly of psychological life. One may "lose oneself in the group," so to speak.[1] Therefore, feuding may be a return to an earlier stage in the "maturation" of vengeance.

So far, Hamlet represents to us the most advanced stage in the process of civilizing vengeance. His internalization of the societal conflicts of his time (which were, by the way, variants of a feuding process) paved the way for a social order governed by individuals who had developed a sense of individual responsibility—a sense, we assert, that is a precondition for an effective social order in which people willingly obey. In other words, a sense of individual responsibility is a precondition for the "social contract."

We saw how, when Hamlet internalized the inherent conflicts of vengeance—the demand that a murder be avenged, the necessity for him to justify killing in the name of "justice"—an inevitable procrastination followed. Hamlet's psychology was a classic case of "ambivalence."

We can also describe these conflicts in terms of a political economy. At the psychological level, for example, some neo–Freudians have described the constant flux and tenuous resolution of internal conflicts as a political economy of the psyche, as though there was just so much energy within the human soul so that it must be apportioned carefully. If too much is apportioned to one particular aspect (e.g., the consummation of vengeance), there is the danger of the individual "losing control" of his actions. On the other hand, if energy is apportioned equally to all aspects of a conflict, then the individual is unable to act at all (as was Hamlet).[2]

If we look at vengeance at the societal level, we see a political economy of raw power that is constantly in a state of delicate equilibrium, or perhaps more accurately, "societal ambivalence." This ambivalence is apparent in many different aspects of societal use of punishment. The use of the death penalty, for example, is constantly legislated and delegislated.[3] There is a constant fluctuation been societal use of "treatment" as against "punishment."[4] But by far the most clearly identifiable flux in the use of vengeance is that of the ebb and flow of feuds. In these social conflicts, we see the direct confrontation of power, resolvable only by the use of power itself, which can be defined as nothing less than raw violence.

There have also been periods in the history of western civilization in which the violence of feuds has been diverted into forms of nonviolent resolution such as compensation. But as we shall see, such conversions were short-lived. These attempts to transform violence into money are particularly informative because they tell much about the political economy of vengeance.

Some Historical Origins of Feuding

Feuding has been identified in various forms in an enormous variety of societies and cultures from the beginning of time to the present. It is probable that all of Europe at some time during the Middle Ages was dominated by feuding as the chief means of imposing justice. Feuding is well documented for the sixth through fourteenth centuries in Europe, especially during the Norman and Frankish periods. There were periodic attempts to limit the blood feuds, but these, while successful for a short time, were ultimately unable to stem the constant ebb and flow of feuding in the Middle Ages.

It was the Frankish empire that introduced the notion of compensation. However, while the notion of amends for injury may be regarded as a considerable advance in the direction of a nonviolent settlement of wrongs, it would be mistaken to suppose that any of the measures aimed at the discouragement of the feud were the fruit of a new and extensive social objective intended to substitute for kinsmen's revenge. Instead, the notion of compensation was embraced by the king because it offered pecuniary advantages to the state. When the state began to enter as an arbitrator between two conflicting parties, part of the compensation was given to the arbitrator as a payment for services rendered.[5]

With the development of the king's law in the Lex Salica, an attempt was made both to undermine the feuding process, but at the same time to embrace certain aspects of it, so as to have it serve the purposes of the state. This was achieved by the introduction of the concept of individual responsibility into the limited criminal code of the time (the earliest criminal offense was probably a "breach of the peace"),[6] and by the kings themselves taking over the administration of vengeance by asserting the right to bring criminal prosecution and by overseeing the process of private prosecution.[7]

There were good reasons why the Frankish kings sought to control the feuding process. The intense loyalty that kinship members shared with each other threatened the developing concept of the divine right, which demanded unqualified obedience and allegiance. Thus, in offering alternatives to the feud, especially when the state could manipulate these options, the Frankish Kingdom was able to shift loyalty from the kinship group to the king. In this way, the demand for reciprocity was short-circuited, so that the king would become the only legitimate avenger, not only in the eyes of God but also in the eyes of the masses of peasants. Thus, the Frankish kings attempted to weave a thread of unity among the divided principalities. But the steady progression toward a unified empire did not eventuate.

The Frankish empire itself began to decay primarily because of the severe economic circumstances that overtook Europe by the tenth century. Compensation was no longer expected to be sufficient to end a feud, simply because the parties involved did not have the wealth to pay.[8]

With the breakdown of the compensatory system feuding returned, but this time in more virulent form. The Frankish kings had tried to make each principality stronger in an effort to bring it closer to the empire, but now the opposite occurred, since each principality began to fight the other. By the tenth century, the feud was no longer a guerilla affair between opposing sides, but rather a form of warfare between military bands. The object of criminal prosecution was no longer peace and order, but the creation of fiscal prerogatives for whoever held jurisdiction. Finally, the Norman invasions dragged on for over three-quarters of a century and the destruction was devastating. It is clear that a system of law that looked to settlement by fixed payments of some tangible value could not be maintained under these conditions. One without chattels could not pay the thirty shillings that the Lex Salica demanded for injuring a man severely, let alone two thousand for homicide.[9]

There is little doubt that scarcity is one of the prime causes of feuding. This may be observed in many parts of the world (the Middle East is perhaps the prototypical), but it also occurs close to home. The feuds in the poverty-stricken Ozarks in the American south are well known. The constant wars between juvenile gangs in the inner urban areas of the United States are feuds as well. These are desolate areas and provide the necessary precondition for the development of feuding.[10]

Feuding in the Middle East

Blood feud in the Middle East has displayed an incredible resistance to change despite the influence of foreign systems of law. While its origin and persistence are no doubt related to the severe economic circumstances of the desolate areas of the Middle East, the blood feud has special religious origins in pre–Islamic Arabia.[11]

In pre–Islamic times, numerous gods and spirits were believed to influence a man's fate. Sacred oaths and blood sacrifices were a means to quell and pacify these spirits. The soul was envisaged as a force that left the body upon death. It was believed to reside in the blood or in the breath so that when death arrived, it escaped through the mouth.

In the case of murder, blood and the need for expiation assumed vital importance. The soul of the murdered man was thought to flutter around the tomb in the form of an owl crying with thirst and unable to rest until vengeance was done. If vengeance was not pursued, then blood guilt fell upon the remaining kin.[12] The idea of revenge or "thar" became a religious obligation from which a basic code of conduct evolved. For instance, an avenger could not kill a man in his sleep because the soul was not present.[13] At the moment of striking the mortal blow, the avenger had to cry aloud that he was taking vengeance for his murdered kinsman so as to inform any witnesses that this was a judicial killing and not an unjustified attack.[14]

Although in theory one man paid for the death of another, thus extinguishing the blood feud, unbridled revenge often reigned. Therefore, certain religious and social customs were observed, which served to maintain social order. For four months of the year, it was accepted that absolute peace should reign. During the spring month of "rajab," even murderers were safe from execution of the blood feud. Murderers would often try to claim the protection of another powerful tribe when the four months were over. The sheikh or head of this protector tribe was often called upon to help arrange an eventual settlement. If proof of the original act was uncertain, the two parties might agree that the avenger should bring a formal accusation against the suspect, who in turn, would take an oath and perform purificatory acts before the assembled notables. Under this rudimentary legal procedure, as many of the accused's kinsmen as possible swore solemnly that the accused had not committed the act. If any one of them refused to do so, the accused was found guilty. The elements of this procedure, particularly as a means of defense, were later incorporated into Islamic law by Mohammed.[15]

There was a choice between exacting vengeance and accepting compensation. Although one could not be forced to accept compensation, and acceptance was indeed regarded as dishonorable, blood money provided a functional means for acquisitions of goods one normally did not possess. The payment of blood money was a collective responsibility, so offenders' kin were also required to pay part of the compensation, or "diya." This alternative remedy transformed blood into *money* rather than honor, thus undermining the "moral" basis of vengeance. That is, it discouraged private vengeance, and hindered the development of individual moral judgment.[16] It was not until Mohammed that the idea of *personal* responsibility became a concept on the *quid pro quo* of crime and punishment.

The Vengeance Code of Islam

As for the thief, both male and female, cut off their hands. It is the reward for their own deeds, an exemplary punishment from Allah.
—*Koran*, V, 38

622 A.D. can be taken as the formal beginning of Islam when Mohammed made his journey from Mecca to Medina. He became the leader of a new religious community with the goal of maintaining internal peace while securing outward expansion. The Constitution of Medina[17] demonstrates vividly the extent to which the Prophet adopted existing legal remedies (such as the blood feud and the demand to match as closely as possible the punishment with the crime), and secured them within a religious framework.[18] The unifying principle of the Islamic constitution lay in its expression of Mohammed's major theme: the formation of a religious community that owes allegiance to divine law as interpreted by God's messenger, the Prophet Mohammed:

The God-fearing believers are against whoever of them acts wrongfully or plans an act that is unjust or treacherous or corrupt among the believers; their hands are all against him, even if he is the son of one of them.[19]

God, no longer the family, became the *only* true avenger. Throughout the Koran, we find that time and time again,

Mohammed had appropriated to himself (and hence to God) the right to exact punishments in the Mosaic tradition. While the matching of injury for injury had become a part of feuding, now it became a part of the "criminal code" as outlined in the holy Koran. At first, Mohammed had tried to eradicate the old tribal divisions completely, but later on in his teachings, it is obvious that he realized the strength and potency of family ties and decided to utilize this energy to his benefit.

> When anyone kills a believer, the evidence being clear, then he is liable to be killed in retaliation for him, unless the representative of the murdered man is satisfied. The believers are against him entirely; nothing is permissible to them except to oppose him.[20]

The phrase "unless the representative of the murdered man is satisfied" epitomizes the crucial weakness of society to impose limitations on revenge. The decision as to what type of vengeance was to be taken, along with the power to execute, remained with the family. Mohammed was certainly still relying on the pre–Islamic machinery of feuding as a source of strength. And it can be seen from the Koran quoted at the beginning of this chatper, that the heir of the victim is explicitly given the right to extract vengeance in response to murder.

The movement from desert society to an empire made it increasingly difficult to look at the tribe as the unit responsible for collective payment of blood money.[21] People, as they became more anonymous to one another, began to make God their avenger. Mohammed, God's avenger on earth, dictated which punishment should be reciprocated for which offense.

The notion of individual wrong-doing without kinship responsibility developed further with the religious idea of guilt. The individualization of responsibility was essentially based upon the growing unity of Islam. All believers now formed a state against the offender who forfeited the protection that would otherwise have been due him by the blood feud.

An attack upon another individual was actually an attack upon the whole community. The response to an offense could no longer be leveled at the individual's kinsmen, but only to the actual offender himself. Murderers were therefore obliged to pay the agreed "diya" on their own.

As the idea of individual responsibility for the crime and the punishment strengthened, so did the character of public punishment. According to official theory the state existed solely for the purpose of putting divine law into effect. The state could execute only measures carefully defined by Shari's law.[22] In practice, however, the responsibilities of government imposed a more active role following the swift rise of the various Arab Emirates. Soon the right to execute vengeance became the right merely to request the public authority to do so.[23] The legal justification given for this by the state came from the principle of *lex talionis*—an eye for an eye, a tooth for a tooth—Mosaic law. And to guard against the possibility that a private individual might exceed the boundaries of revenge, the public authorities decided to carry out the task themselves. Today, vengeance cultures of the Middle East still persist among the more isolated nomadic tribes.

In Italy, there are other vengeance cultures with rich codes of conduct and frightening traditions of violence. In these cultures, vengeance has taken on different forms because of unique historical and geographical conditions. One such culture is the Mafia and its various counterparts found in southern Italy. However, because of its specially "abnormal" attributes, we will reserve discussion of this type of vengeance culture until chapter 9. Quite different from the Mafia organizations, is the culture of vengeance found in the interior of Sardinia. Here we find one of the classic feuding cultures of southern and eastern Europe.

The Feud in Sardinia

> Hocchire toccat a Deus
> (Killing is the task only of God)
> —A Sardinian saying.

It was a mild afternoon in September 1959, in Sedilo, a small village in the interior of Sardinia.[24] The Carabinieri (Italy's military police), on the basis of a tip-off, were reconnoitering the nearby countryside.

They quickly discovered the bloody corpses of a man and two women, victims of a ferocious ambush. Even though the police were used to the sight of bloody murders, the scene that they came upon was horrendous, even to them. The corpse of the man lying on his back, arms open, was completely riddled with bullets, the face totally disfigured. Many of the shots had been fired from a shotgun at close range to the face.[25]

The methodical and rapid action inflicted on the victims

was clearly apparent, even though the typical mutilations such as particular slashes to the throat, were absent. (It has been quite common in Sardinia to cut off the ears for cattle theft because according to ancient tradition, the cattle were branded on the ears. It was also common to cut the throat or the mouth from ear to ear for spies—again, with clear symbolic or reflexive purpose.)[26] There was no doubt that this was an example of "cold, homicidal anger," typical of the murder of vengeance.

This multiple murder, known as "the murder of Lacunas" (Lacunas being the location of the killing), was the climax of a "Disamistade," one of the wildest feuds in Sardinian history.[27] Here, Titino Falchi, the recognized leader of one faction, lost his life, as did his wife and sister-in-law, whose presence at the moment of the attack was not enough to prevent the killers from doing their terrible deed.

The story of this feud and of the protagonist of the other faction, Peppino Pes, demonstrates some typical traits of conflict between clans in those times, traits that endure even today. Toward the end of the 1940s, two clans in the same village competed with each other for influence over the surrounding areas.[28] Each of the two extended families, according to its position of power, acquired a number of allied clans that enabled it to influence larger and larger portions of the village inhabitants. Thus, when the hostility began, the population was already set for a split, each to support its respective clan.

Even though the two factions came from a common cultural background, there were differences, especially when we consider the characters of the two leaders. Titino Falchi, leader of the Falchi faction, is described as an "old fashioned boss" with a fatherly attitude. He was clever in the administration of family business, namely, the progressive accumulation of money and power by trafficking in stolen cattle, a traditional criminal activity common to the pastoral areas of inner Sardinia. Notwithstanding his premier position of superiority in comparison to the other clans, Falchi attempted for the first time to include the Pes clan within his own organization—in a more subordinate position, of course. This was an attempt to avoid a possible feud.

Peppino Pes, who was a much younger leader, was considerably different from Falchi and from other leaders in that he was much more educated, having been a student in a seminary. (It is even said that he had once seriously considered the priesthood.) However, his father was killed in a barroom argument so the family's business was subsequently administered by his mother, a very strong and dominant woman.[29]

By the time Peppino was 21, he had already committed a number of serious crimes for which he was never convicted. His youth and the relative weakness of the family began to disturb the equilibrium between the two clans. His criminal activity threatened to interfere with the business activity of the Falchi clan, although there was yet no open hostility between them.

The classic beginning of hostility came from the strongest clan. Falchi tipped the police off as to the whereabouts of the fugitive Peppino Pes, who was subsequently captured and very seriously wounded. Miraculously, he escaped death, and after four years in prison came back to his village, absolved of all charges. On his return, he made a formal "declaration of war" against the Falchi clan by refusing to shake the hand of their leader Titino, and making an open allusion to his wound, which waited to be avenged. Titino, in a classic gesture of reciprocity, returned the insult, recalling to Peppino that he still had to avenge the death of his father, before he could even consider avenging himself.

The real feud was then previewed by a series of classic reciprocal minor offenses between the clans such as cattle stealing and the publication of lists of spies who were to be killed. But the feud formally began in February 1954.

The first victim was Lussorio Mongili of the Falchi faction, shot down near his village. This first episode was the beginning of an impressive sequel of reciprocal homicides. The police, in an attempt to prevent further crimes, sent Peppino Pes to the small island of Ustica, close to Palermo, where he was to remain in "compulsory residence,"[30] even though he had not been convicted of any crimes.

During this time, when the Pes clan was temporarily weakened by the absence of its leader, an episode of gravity took place that made it impossible for any subsequent agreement to stop the bloodshed. On the afternoon of January 26, 1956, Antonietta Deiana, Pes's mother, was wounded by the shot of a handgun fired through the door of her house. Although she probably recognized the aggressor, she gave misleading information to the police in order to reserve for her son the right to avenge the assailant.

From this moment on, the feud escalated without limit. A short time after the attempted murder of the mother, the lieutenant of the Falchi faction, Giovanni Battista Falchi, was killed. The particular ferocity of this homicide suggested that this victim had been the one who had tried to kill Pes's mother. Peppino's return to the village after his enforced exile was immediately followed by the killing of another member of the Falchi faction, Francesco Angelo Mongili.

At this point, it became clear that the intention of Pes was to annihilate the entire Falchi faction, or if not, to force it out of the area. Even though the military and police patrolled the villages and surrounding areas twenty-four hours a day, and the leaders of the clans were under constant surveillance, this was not enough to prevent an attempt against Peppino Pes. A killer named Pasquale Solinas ambushed him, but was only able to kill his horse, leaving Pes unharmed.

The Falchis were now beginning to feel their losses, and consequently, because of their relative weakness, they again tried to deal with the Pes clan through official channels—the police. They tried to get Pes arrested and prosecuted but this plot failed because Pes's influence on the witness brought forward by the Falchis was much too strong.

Pes's next task was to settle his account with Solinas who had tried to kill him. On a night in January 1957, as Solinas was approaching his home, a shadowy figure suddenly appeared, pointed a shotgun into his face, and killed him. Another Pes enemy was dead. At this point, the Falchi faction was forced into retreat, its old leader trying any way he could to obtain the capture of Peppino, now a fugitive because he had been finally convicted of the murder of Solinas. In his last days, the old boss lived in fear.

> Falchi, almost entirely isolated, lived in severe anxiety because of his fear of being killed by the Pes.[31]

The same fear forced almost all the Falchi supporters to flee from the village, especially after the pitiless and multiple execution of Lacunas. But not everybody was able to get out in time, with the result that they would fall, one after the other, victims of the vengeful hatred of Pes. The systematic chain of

executions is a familiar technique,[32] the goal being to amplify
fear. There are ambushes. Victims are first wounded, until the
last shot, almost touching the face is fired from the shotgun.
While the Pes clan's victory was almost won, the leader's time
was, nevertheless, running out.

This feud, because of its wildness and ferocity, had become
a subject of national interest. It seemed impossible during the
"civilized" sixties that such a private war over which the state
had no control could take place. More extraordinary was the
fact that the state was used by both of the factions to achieve
their own ends. A reward of three million lire offered by the
authorities was eventually sufficient to encourage one of the
Pes clan to betray the invisible Peppino, who, in spite of
everything, had lived for several years within the village.
Peppino, caught in a house that was practically next to the
local police station, is now serving a life sentence in a medium
security prison in Siena, and is considered to be a model
prisoner. There have even been many pleas to have him
released on the grounds of his good behavior.

The feud that we have briefly described demonstrates some
classic elements of a vengeful exchange between two opposing factions. The source of the conflict was genuinely economic and political. But the most important factor was the
loss of equilibrium between the two factions, and this was
perceived as "unjust" by the weaker faction. Thus, each
fought to establish its monopoly over honor. Both elements of
vengeance that we have previously outlined are clearly
present: the quest for reciprocity, and the means by which this
may be attained, which is coercion. A surplus of vengeance
produced by a series of escalating affronts to honor was
another outcome.

The predominant faction was not about to share its control
of economic resources. There were sound economic reasons
for not doing so, and the traditional practice of cattle stealing
in a nomadic and somewhat predatory society is itself proof of
the mental agility and physical abilities of the clan.[33] We must
also consider that this activity was taken up during the time
when the other faction was weak (because of the death of the
father), and so the Falchis took advantage of the Pes clan
during its time of weakness.

The character of the old leader of the Falchi, and the
principle of authority that he represented, are easily under-

stood as a possible source of oppression. In reality, he was an obstacle to the acquisition of power desired by the youthful Peppino. This is a familiar pattern, similar to those of the classic myths that we have described. It is also typical of classic vengeance that in order to initiate hostilities, a precipitating offense must occur giving "justification" for reprisals. Furthermore, this precipitating incident must be perpetrated by the authority figure, in this case the father or leader of the clan.

We also notice that during the development of the feud, each side successively was in a position of relative weakness, so that it perpetrated a massive act of violence in order to overcome this weakness. In other words, the weaker the position, the more violent the reaction or reprisal, and the more likely the response of "overkill."

It is clear that, even though seemingly uncontrolled violence erupted, these acts of violence were nevertheless carried out according to certain rules and patterns. This code of conduct has reached a sophisticated level in Sardinia, so that it forms the core of the culture of the island's interior.

The Sardinian Code of Vengeance

> Su sambene no est abba. (Blood is not water)
> —A Sardinian saying.

In Sardinia, the presence of a long established code of vengeance that displays a high degree of formalization and seems, to this day, to regulate the mechanism of the feuds as well as individual vengeance, has been analyzed by Antonio Pigliaru. It has been interpreted as an expression of the wider discrepancy between cultural models of the inner areas of the island and that of Italian society in general. This hypothesis was stated some years ago in the now classic book by Wolfgang and Ferracuti, *The Subculture of Violence.*

Because of its unique history and culture, a particular lifestyle has been maintained in the inner areas of Sardinia that serves to regulate and control violent behavior.[34] The state, traditionally viewed by the inhabitants as a source of "foreign" domination, was always immersed in conflict with the local inhabitants. Historically, in fact, this authority has been sporadic and essentialy remote. This condition of conflict, linked to the permanent social organization of extended families and clans that were also in conflict with each other for control of territory and goods, has produced, over the centuries, a climate of isolation and antagonism towards external forces of change. It is not then surprising that the Sardinian pastoral society has developed a system of defining and controlling conflict by avoiding any recourse to a third party—i.e., the state. We can see that this is an attempt to maintain social order without resorting to the obedience model.

The antagonism between the two models of reciprocity and obedience that we have proposed to explain the phenomenon of vengeance is also clear if we consider this customary code, and in general, the conflict between a pastoral subculture and the wider Italian culture. The culture of vengeance that underlies this code is also responsible, at least in part, for the mechanism of identification and support of bandit figures that are opposed to the pressing external cultural forces. In this context, the code seems to express the need of the pastoral society to exercise a limitation and control on the destructive mechanism of vengeful exchange. In order to do this, the code must be able to define offensive and vengeful action in terms of crimes and punishments. It must be able to establish "objective" limitations to vengeful behavior beyond the definitions of offense given by each party or faction.

The Offenses

According to the code of vengeance, "one determinate action is offensive when the event from which depends the existence of such offense is foreseen in order to damage dignity and honor."[35] Property damage in itself is not an offense, and is not sufficient cause for vengeance unless it were done with specific intent to offend the honor of the clan or individual. In this case the offensive will is determined by the basis of objective circumstances or subjective circumstances such as the intensity of malice and condition of the offender, or the relation between the offender and offended.[36]

A good example of this kind of property offense, which according to the code of vengeance is a "real" offense, was the killing of the Pes's cattle by Pasquale Solinas. This action was set up in order to elicit an offensive damage, which was achieved, because it was perpetrated by a person whose relation with the offended faction was of open enmity.[37]

In addition, the code of vengeance considers other kinds of offenses of different degrees of gravity. The most serious offense is murder. Other offenses are bearing false witness and spying.[38] The code states clearly that the collective or individual responsibility is the constitutive element of the offense itself. In fact, according to "article 5" of the code, the responsibility for the offensive action is individual or collective according to whether the offense follows the action of a single person or that of a group that is operating as a group. The group is organized according to family structure, and is not responsible for the offenses when they are produced by a single member of the group. Only when the group expresses clear and active solidarity in favor of the culprit, is collective responsibility seen as part of the offense.

Antonio Pigliaru has observed that intentionality is the essential element of the offenses because vengeance, at this stage in its development (i.e. focused on the original offender, rather than unfocused like that of Achilles), must be intentional in order to be directed to the proper source of offense.

Therefore, the offenses can be extinguished only when the "victim/offender" recognizes his responsibility, and takes on himself the charge to repay the "debt" that is "requested" by the offended person, or, when the offender acts in a situation in which he has no other choice (e.g. where he is forced by violence), in which case the author of the violence is responsible for the offense. Once it is stated that the offense is an act set up in order to damage the honor of the other, we must determine exactly what it means to damage the dignity and honor of another.

Pigliaru says that the intent of the offender is either to annihilate or return to a position of weakness the other person or family by hitting them at their weakest point. For example, the use of arson makes clear that there is no material gain from the offense, but ensures that the other faction is placed at a loss. The intent to injure the other party is therefore clear. It is to upset the reciprocity and balance of power between the two factions by taking advantage of the weakness of the other, trying to impose authority with violence, and annihilate the enemy by violent means. The offense is, in this way, similar to, and derivative of, the primitive feeling that we identified at the beginning of this book, of being arbitrarily subjected to a tyrannical power against which one seems powerless to act.

The Punishment

Article 1 of the vengeance code states that vengeance is obligatory. The offenses MUST be avenged.[39] Once the collective or individual responsibility for the offense has been proven, the law of vengeance obliges all persons concerned to take revenge.[40] Obviously, the primary responsibility for implementing vengeance is with the offended person or group. In the Sardinian code, vengeance consists essentially of an offense that is given in response to that which was received. This offense should, in its classic form, match the precipitating offense in kind, but may nevertheless return more damage than was received. The vengeful act should be proportional, but progressive.

We have observed that this tendency of vengeful exchange leads, within the limits of progressive graduation, to the extreme form of retaliation, which is blood vengeance i.e. murder as revenge. The extreme difficulty in reaching a peaceful resolution to the conflict is most evident when, in blood vengeance, one is required to avenge a previous homicide. Predictably, bloody offenses are the only ones for which the code provides no "statute of limitations." Murders are never forgotten. In this way, the limitless "market" for vengeance is perpetuated. The punishment of blood vengeance is inflicted not only for homicides, but also for crimes "against honor," such as breaking a promise of marriage, spying, and bearing false witness.

The progressive tendency of vengeful exchange is clear; the offense that has acted as vengeance in itself constitutes a new offense which should be avenged. Blood vengeance in particular is a capital offense, even though it is given in order to avenge a preceeding blood offense. In this instance we see the classic basis of what outsiders are inclined to call "chaos." It is a society in which there is no way to distinguish between crimes and punishments. They are, in fact, interchangeable, equally justifiable, equally criminal.

In recognizing the two elements of proportionality and

responsibility (personal and collective) in vengeance, the code seems to be an evolution in comparison with the old conception of vengeance in which the retaliation was automatically and mechanically inflicted on all the members of the offender group. However, the maturation of vengeance is not quite as advanced as it was in Hamlet. That is to say, the societal and cultural form of vengeance is not as "primitive" a form of social control as it seems at first glance. Rather, it seems to be halfway between the primitive and the civilized. On the one hand, it does provide the basic distinctions that most established legal codes provide, such as the analysis of intent, the distinction of individual and collective responsibility; but on the other hand the mechanism of control is unable to go the full way of pronouncing which of the acts is criminal and which is not. To attain this, we need a "civilized" society in which a third party—the state—is able to transcend the opposing factions and pronounce which acts are criminal and which are not. It is apparent in feuding societies that the opposing factions will even join together in order to oppose a third party, almost invariably perceived as foreign and representative of an illegitimate order.

The pastoral society of Sardinia, in its warlike attitude, represents an interesting example, rare in western society, of the problems related to the regulation of social conflict, especially the maintenance of a permanent but unstable "equilibrium," without resort to an external principle authority. According to the Sardinian code, more than what could be done, must be done. The necessity to reap vengeance is also more than a private duty. Rather, it is a public duty in the sense that it must be performed on behalf of a code that is adhered to by both factions. The community is served by each side carrying out its duty to avenge. The avenger will even consider revenge as a necessary and unavoidable destiny from which there is no escape. The existence of rigid and immovable rules is typical of any traditional society. The wonder of vengeance is that, in this context, it provides the moral basis for the social order. Vengeance reveals itself as a kind of violence that eradicates the moral damage that was the consequence of another act of violence—a violence that cancels out each previous act, yet recreates itself. It is just as Marx analyzed capital. It works wonders, creating new commodities, which in turn, through social exchange, recreate capital.

Notes

1. It will be recognized that this is a variant of Freud's theory as expounded in S. Freud, *Group Psychology and Analysis of the Ego*, trans. J. Strachey (New York: Bantam, 1960).

2. This perspective was introduced by Freudian revisionists essentially because they sought to achieve an important theoretical breakthrough; they wanted to make direct links between psychological conflicts and societal conflicts. The major proponent of this approach was Wilhelm Reich. See W. Reich, *The Mass Psychology of Fascism*, trans. V. Carfagno (New York: Farrar, Straus and Giroux, 1970). And for a somewhat less Freudian approach, R. D. Laing, *The Politics of Experience* (New York: Ballantine, 1967).

3. See Graeme Newman, *The Punishment Response* (New York: Lippincott, 1978).

4. See G. Newman, *Just and Painful* (New York: Macmillan, 1983). On our culture's inherent ambivalence towards the use of violence, see also the captivating book by R. Girard, *Violence and the Sacred* (Baltimore: Johns Hopkins University Press, 1977).

5. See Julius Goebel, Jr., *Felony and Misdemeanor: A Study in the History of Criminal Law* (Pennsylvania: University of Pennsylvania Press, 1976), pp. xix, 1–9; J. M. Wallace-Hadrill, *The Long-Haired Kings and Other Studies in Frankish History* (London: Methuen and Co., 1959).

6. The concept of individual responsibility is of considerable interest during this period. The individual acquired legal importance only through his membership and continued association in a group. Membership in this group was an "honor" *(mannhelgi*, see Goebel, p. 9), and if an individual broke this honor (for instance by stealing within the group) this was a breach of the peace, the punishment for which was exclusion from the group.

7. See R. Latovche, *Les origines de l'économie occidentale*, 1956, p. 41, cited in Goebel, *Felony and Misdemeanor*, pp. 2–10.

8. See Goebel. p. 195. The charters of the late tenth and early eleventh centuries indicate that compensation was no longer considered a substitute or a means of ending feud. This is attributable to the decay of material wealth that could not support a system of compensation involving material commodities. The tariffed compensation had been almost completely engulfed in the maelstrom of a warrior's society. Among the Germanic tribes, the reckoning of a man's *wergeld*, was based upon the assumptions as to the normal economic situation of a particular group of kinsmen. Compensation as an alternative to feuding cannot sustain itself if persons are without substance to make a trade-off. Thus, it is probable that the complete decline of the system in the tenth and eleventh centuries was due to the decline of material abundance. From the year 970 to 1040, there were over forty-eight years of famine in France. See Mark Bloch *Feudal Society* (Chicago: University of Chicago Press, 1961).

9. Ibid., p. 268.

10. See I. C. Horowitz, and G. Schwartz, "Honor, Normative Ambiguity and Gang Violence," *American Sociological Review*, 39 (1974): 238–51.

11. M. J. L. Hardy, *Blood Feud and the Payment of Blood Money in the Middle East* (Leiden: E. J. Brill, 1963) p. 14.

12. Ibid., p. 20.

13. Ibid., p. 19.

14. Ibid., p. 19.

15. Ibid., p. 23.

16. This is not to say, however, that honor did not play an important part in Middle East feuds. It has remained Central for many important reasons. See Hardy, *Blood Feud*, ibid; Peristiany, J. G. (ed.) *Honour and Shame: the Values of Mediterranean Society* (London: Weidenfeld and Nicolson, 1965); and Jane Schneider, "Of vigilance and virgins: honor, shame and access to resources in Mediterranean societies," *Ethnology*, 10 (1971): 1–24.

17. A translation of this constitution is contained in W. A. H. Montgomery, *Mohammed at Medina* (Oxford: Clarendon Press, 1953), p. 192.

18. G. Newman, Khomeini and Criminal Justice: Notes on Crime and Culture, *Journal of Criminal Law and Criminology*, 73 (1982): 2, 561–81.

19. Article 36 of the constitution of Medina, *Mohammed at Medina*, ibid.

20. Ibid., article 21.

21. Hardy, p. 31.

22. Shari'a law is the term used to describe the body of religious proscriptions and enjoinders composed of tradition, custom, and the Koran itself. It is generally considered to have been well developed into four distinct schools by the end of the ninth century A.D. See Fazlur Rahman: *Islam* (London: Weidenfeld and Nicolson, 1966).

23. Ibid., p. 46.

24. Sardinia, as professor Wolgang pointed out in his significant introduction to *Violence in Sardinia*, is one of the most culturally isolated islands in Western Europe. Sedilo is a village located on the fringe of the area known as Barbagia—named by the ancient Romans for its wild and isolated character. Sedilo shares the cultural traditions of the wild area, including the typical criminal activities of its inhabitants, cattle stealing. See P. Marongiu, *Teoria e storia del banditismo sociale in Sardegna* (Cagliari: Edizioni Della Torre, 1981), p. 167: also F. Ferracuti, R. Lazzari, and M. Wolfgang, *Violence in Sardinia* (Rome: Bulzoni, 1970), p. 9.

25. An accurate report of this episode and the entire feud is reported in A. Ledda, *La civiltà fuorilegge* (Milano: Mursia, 1971), pp. 127–150.

26. The reflexive element of punishment in the offense often occurs in blood vengeance murders. Although, in general, the ordinary people may interpret these mutilations as having a deterrent effect, we are more inclined to interpret them as retributive in nature when they occur in the feud, since we have shown that they tend to have an escalating effect rather than a deterrent effect on the violence. This is somewhat different from its use by the Mafia, as we will see later, where its use is quite specifically aimed at deterrence, and achieving an effective social control.

27. The term *Disamistade* derives, according to different interpretations, from the ancient Italian or Spanish language, and can be translated roughly as the opposite of friendship—enmity. It indicates the very process of the feud with its typical interchange of violent acts.

28. Both families had their origin in the land-owning class, an origin, however, relatively recent following the "Editto delle Chiudende" of October 1820, which authorized the private ownership of land by creating

enclosures of the land that was previously in common use. This created a tremendous change in the social and economic structure of the island because it introduced a class differentiation into the society.

29. In the family structure of Sardinia, although the paternal figure is the formally recognized authority, the mother figure usually exercises much power because of her traditional role in a society in which the men are away from the village for long periods of time tending their sheep and cattle. The wife therefore maintains social relations and is very active in social life. In the case of the Pes family, the death of the father reinforced this tendency.

30. In Italian law, this is usually the legal confinement within a particular village.

31. See A. Ledda, *La civiltà fuorilegge*, (Milano: Mursia, 1971) p. 141.

32. Modern terrorists whose goals are political have adopted this method throughout the world. Terrorist methods and styles can be traced to feuding and banditry, as we will see in the following chapter. The method is also used by the Mafia, as we will see in chapter 9.

33. These qualities together constitute a cultural pattern called *balentia*, the ability to face the difficulties of life with courage, intelligence, responsibility.

34. Antonio Pigliaru, professor of law at the University of Sassari, Sardinia, conducted a complex research project that examined the official trial transcripts of feuds, bandits, and criminality, with an analysis of newspapers over a period of fifty years, and extensive field research. The result of this project was a formulation of a code of vengeance that according to his view, still operates in certain internal areas of Sardinia. See A. Pigliaru, "*La Vendetta Barbaricina Come Ordinamento Giuridico in Il banditismo in Sardegna*, (Milano: Giuffre, 1975); also M. E. Wolfgang and F. Ferracuti, *The Subculture of Violence* (London: Tavistock, 1967); F. Ferracuti, R. Lazzari, and M. E. Wolfgang, *Violence in Sardinia*.

35. A. Pigliaru, *La Vendetta barbaricina come ordinamento giuridico*, p. 119.

36. Article 14 of the code of vengeance recognizes an offense in the following case of property damage: (a) cattle stealing: when perpetrated by an enemy, by a former partner of the shepherd who is acquainted with the his partner's movements, or by a neighbor, or if made possible by their complicity, (b) stealing of a she-goat in milk when it is used to support the family, (c) stealing of a pig when it is used to support the family economy, (d) stealing of livestock or cutting the the hocks of horses or oxen used for everyday work. See A. Pigliaru, *La Vendetta*, pp. 121–22.

37. Further relevant "offenses" in the code are: (e) injury and killing of cattle, (f) arson, (g) stealing or cutting the hocks of a milk cow which is a gift for a newborn child, wife, or orphan, (h) illegal or unauthorized use of pasture which is enclosed, done with the intent to provoke or with spite, (i) unjust patrimonial division of inheritance when it is done to take advantage of someone who, at the moment of division, was not in condition to assert his right, (l) excessive implementation of one's rights. See A. Pigliaru, *La Vendetta*, pp. 121–22.

38. Other offenses are, according to article 16 of the code (moral offenses): (a) provocative trespass on enclosed land, (b) insult, (c) defamation and calumny, (d) breaking of a promise of marriage. This offense is aggra-

vated when this aggravation is done with the intent to publicly damage the honor of the girl or her family, (e) unjustified breaking or failure to fulfill an agreement, (f) spying, (g) bearing false witness, (h) insult or act against a guest, (i) blood offense. See A. Pigliaru, *La Vendetta*, pp. 123–24.

39. Ibid., article 1, p. 111.

40. From this point of view, no one who lives in the community should suffer vengeance unless it is absolutely clear that he was responsible for one of these classified offenses. See Pigliaru, *La Vendetta*, pp. 114–115.

7

The Political Economy of Vengeance

La lesive de l'honner ne secoule qu au sang.
(The laundry of honor is only bleached by blood).[1]

Total Scarcity: The Economic Base of Feuding

In Marx's political and economic theory, the competition for scarce resources is of central importance. However, he gave little attention, if any, to the idea of *total* scarcity, a condition of special significance to feuding, and one that requires an adaptation of Marx's theory if we are to make sense of the violence and social organization of feuding.

While the essential motivating force in feuds is that of revenge, it is a mistake to conclude that vengeance causes feuds. Rather, there are many conditions that are conducive to feuds, and that serve to intensify the desire for vengeance. Anthropologists and historians have emphasized a number of themes that appear to be related to feuds in general, and to the formation of codes of vengeance in particular. By far, the most important of these is the phenomenon of total scarcity.[2] The anthropologist Black-Michaud summarizes total scarcity as

> the moral, institutional and material presence of a certain type of society in which everything felt by the people themselves to be relevant to human life is regarded by those people as existing in absolute inadequate quantities.[3]

The feud, being a response to conditions of total scarcity, produces a surrogate social system that ameliorates institutional deficiencies caused by a constellation of ecological and historical variables. This process gives rise to a special form of social organization and unique cultural styles.

Total scarcity can occur in any society at any time depending upon the availability, production, and exploitation of material goods and resources. It develops in societies whose materials are so scarce that social organizations are affected in every aspect by the resulting precarious subsistence economy. It maintains a decisive influence upon patterns of social organization designed to facilitate group survival. Survival, during conditions of material scarcity, becomes a group struggle.[4] Individual moral judgments are thus inhibited from developing.

The existence of scarcity of resources automatically creates a situation of social conflict over the meagerness of that which is available. Employing Coser's working definition of social conflict, "a struggle over values and claims to scarce status, power and resources,"[5] we find that the feud adequately fits this description. The very notion of conflict, as Coser intimates, is a function of the law of supply and demand. Conflict arises when two or more parties enter into a competitive struggle to gain control of the "prize" of which there exists an insufficient supply to satisfy the demands of all contestants. The unavailability of basic resources in quantities ample enough to satisfy all those who require them represents the factor of scarcity.[6] In the face of such fierce competition (one thinks of the "war of all against all"), how do feuding clans become so cohesive?

Fear: The Binding Force

Mutual aid and defense relationships develop from the most important concomitant of scarcity—*fear*. Fear of starvation due to the individual's incapacity to defend his resources against aggression is prevalent among feuding societies of the Mediterranean. In conditions of total scarcity, groups of people form alliances to create balance, which is maintained through the process of feud, with the view to securing an equal distribution of available resources. Fear of foreign invasion, which threatens not only one's resources but can destroy cultural identity as well, has spawned the growth of the feud as a self-help institution. This activity is common in societies in Albania, the Middle East, and parts of Italy, which have for centuries, resisted any external influence, and have, in fact, repelled attempts at invasion.[7]

Fear, as Black-Michaud points out, is the ultimate motive for alliance.[8] Fear of aggression promotes equalitarian alliances to create a balance of forces in the face of potential anarchy. If fear of aggression were removed in societies of this type, organization into a series of evenly matched coalitions would no longer be necessary and the system would then fall apart. If, on the other hand, aggression knew no limits and no alliances were formed to check the spread of violence, the Hobbesian war of all against all would reign.

Seen in this light, feud constitutes the main *organizational* principle of all the feuding societies of the Mediterranean and the Middle East. Fear maintains the social system while at the same time constituting a permanent threat to peace and order. In acephalous societies in which threats to survival knit the society into a tissue of relationships based on alliance and balanced opposition, "fear of incurring a blood-feud . . . is the most important legal sanction within a [tribe] and the main guarantee of an individual's life and property."[9] However, the political economy of feuding contains further potential sources of conflict.

Conflict between Authority and Collective Action

Black-Michaud claims that feud constitutes not only a relationship between equals, but also a paradoxical means of affirming authority in the absence of an institutionalized power structure.[10] Equalitarian relationships are not universal within an internal hierarchy, if that hierarchy is built on the basis of something other than material wealth. Members of the group only share an equalitarian outlook as far as distribution of material resources is concerned. This is a necessity in conditions of scarcity when individuals have a fear of starvation. No one may obtain more than his fair share if all are to survive. Therefore, relationships created and maintained through feud are fundamentally ambiguous. Alliances contracted in response to aggression cannot be as uncompromisingly equalitarian in structure and operation as one might assume, for some form of leadership must emerge in order to deal effectively with aggression.

The fact is that in feuding societies one always finds equality and hierarchy side by side. Cooperation and conflict (for leadership) are not mutually exclusive opposites but the poles of a continuing social processs.[11] Cooperation is a necessary prerequisite for the formation of groups, especially in conditions of scarcity where collective effort is imperative for survival. Yet a group cannot continue functioning unless leadership, which naturally assumes an internal hierarchy of competition, emerges to direct the common effort to the accomplishment of the established goal. Leadership, while making cooperation possible, nonetheless stimulates an atmosphere of competition which, if intensified, results in internal conflict. If internal conflict becomes too intense to maintain collective solidarity, the group will divide and the social structure of cooperation, mitigated by competition, will be superseded by direct conflict between opposing fragments. Thus, in spite of the inhibitive effects upon stratification by conditions of total scarcity and the presence of a strong equalitarian ideology, feud will almost always give rise to some form of leadership.[12]

In the absence of material wealth, what other basis is there for the development of a hierarchy that produces leadership? As noted in chapter 1, in a truly primitive society the answer to this question would have been brute force. But feuding societies, as we will see in the following chapters, are not primitive; they are in many respects quite developed. We should therefore expect that in these societies, brute force will have been transformed into something else.

From Scarcity to Abundance: Creating Value from Nothing.

Perhaps the most entertaining and captivating of all Karl Marx's theories was his account of the transformation of the concrete into the abstract—specifically, the dynamic social process by which the concrete labor of men was changed into the highly abstract form of capital—money. Marx's theory pivoted on the careful dissection of the process of economic exchange. He demonstrated how an *equal* exchange was impossible in a capitalistic society, since the participants in the exchange were unequal in the first place. Furthermore, the transformation of matter (labor power) seems to have begun in the dim beginnings of history when man first traded the product of his labor for another commodity. Thus, he alienated himself from his own labor, and allowed a portion of his labor to be "traded" (in psychological terms we might say "objectified.") In any event, this was the beginning of the transformation of concrete labor into its more abstract representations in the forms of various commodities.[13] Marx characterizes this process as almost magical.

The situation of total scarcity removes Marx's first premise: everyone is *equally* poverty stricken. Thus, feuding societies must find another source of magic, since there is no labor power to transform. Indeed, the members of these feuding societies are forced to make something out of nothing.

We know from the work of many anthropologists that hierarchies, that is to say social differentiation, nevertheless develop, but that they are not based on economic differentiation, since there are insufficient resources to allow for such stratification. Rather, prestige, honor, manliness become the referents for social evaluation. Indeed, honor and manliness come to be regarded as *commodities*. It takes little imagination to see that Marx's theory, though it cannot apply literally to feuds since it is so grounded on economic differentiation, can nevertheless be applied to the inequality that exists in terms of honor and manliness. Viewed in this way, the social dynamic of feuding takes on fantastic forms similar to those described by Marx in regard to capitalism.

First, violence is the driving force in every feud. Every exchange is bathed in blood, just as Marx argued that money oozed from the pores of every exchange.[14] In other words, blood is the medium of exchange, not money. (It is no coincidence at all that in periods of feuding when compensatory systems have developed, the compensation was called "blood money.") We may go so far as to say that the venting of blood takes on certain ritualistic, indeed religious forms, in much the same way as Marx describes the capitalist's worship of money. We will see in the following chapter much evidence of these *cultural* expressions of the worship of vengeance.[15]

This analysis also suggests that, in every feuding exchange, there will be a "little blood left over"—a surplus. This occurs first, because the participants in the exchange are unequal in the first place, not materially, but *physically*. Second, there is inherent in the vengeful exchange itself the impossibility of matching exactly the violence of one offense with another.[16]

That is, we must see the value of violence in the feud as a variant of what Marx called *exchange value*. In other words, each act of violence, if it is more severe than the act that provoked it, is assured of a greater satisfaction of vengeance. Therefore, there is the constant tendency to "overkill."[17] It is this impossibility of equal exchange that provides the impetus for a continuation of the feud. It becomes interminable, and can never be completed, except when one side is totally destroyed.

Finally, according to this Marxist model, we should also expect there to be some feuding "capitalists" who will attempt to accumulate the surplus blood that is left over from each exchange. These will be the individuals who become the leaders in vengeance cultures. Blood, however, cannot be saved or hoarded as can money. It must therefore be transformed into a universal commodity like money that can be accumulated and stored, and whose significance or value is *intangible* and *symbolic*. The first step in this transformation of bodily essence is to equate the spilling of blood with the abstract quality of manliness.

The Concept of Honor and the Fetish for Manliness

Honor and shame have often been described as the two universal poles of social evaluation.

> They are the reflection of the social personality in the mirror of social ideals as well as being the apex of the pyramid of temporal social values. They condition a hierarchical order.[18]

Cutting across all other social classifications, honor divides social beings into two fundamental categories: those endowed with honor and those deprived of it. Like material acquisitions, honor becomes a commodity that is strived for in order to achieve a higher status in the social hierarchy. The more scarce the resource, the more important it becomes.

The anthropologist Peristiany explains that honor and shame are the constant preoccupation of individuals in small-scale, exclusive societies where face-to-face, personal encounters, as opposed to anonymous relations, are of paramount importance.[19] Embodied within this evaluative system is the insecurity and instability of the honor-shame ranking, which actually is its perpetual, motivating force. Because of the constant threat to the individual's or group's mental and physical survival, instability forms the foundation for human interaction. Within the cultural sphere, this instability is emphasized by the constant needs of individuals to assert and reassert their honor. Thus, the more one spills blood asserting one's self, the more "honorable" one becomes.

Hobbes once spoke about the existence of a pecking order of honor in societies of "equals,"[20] such as within an agricultural or pastoral community. Within these societies there exists constant competition for the bestowal of honor.[21] The victor in any competition for honor finds his reputation enhanced by the humiliation of the vanquished. In some parts of Italy, it was believed that one who gave an insult thereby took unto himself the reputation of which he deprived another.[22]

Why does honor assume such central importance in feuding societies? Why don't hierarchies develop that are based on altruism rather than the exchange of violence? Altruistic acts, after all, should also engender reciprocity (although the expectation of a reciprocal act of altruism is perhaps a little more questionable).[23] The reason, we think, has to do with the inherent link between honor and power that arises from the intimate relationship between honor and the physical person, and finally the question of personal identity.

To begin with, the rituals by which honor is formally bestowed involve a ceremony that centers upon the head of the protagonist whether it is the crowning of a monarch, or the touch on the head with a book to confer academic degrees in a university. The payment of honor in daily life is accorded through the demonstrations of respect that are commonly associated with the head, whether it is bowed, touched, covered, adorned, or even chopped off. Even where "polite society" has outlawed physical violence, it retains the ritual slap on the face as a challenge to settle an affair.[24]

Any form of physical affront implies an affront to honor since the "ideal sphere" surrounding a person's honor of which Simmel speaks is defiled.[25] The only way that an offense to honor can be redeemed is through the spilling of blood. Honor is thus exalted through the physical person. In contrast to Hamlet, whose identity crisis was brought on by his internal reflection and vacillation on the use of violence, the avenger in feuding societies develops his "identity" directly through violence. The problem of identity is simple for him: "I am whom I kill."

In the context of feuding, this makes for a powerful psychological and social process that virtually knows no limits. As capitalism lives off an ever expanding market, and would die if limits were placed upon it, so too does feuding become interminable.

Bearing in mind Coser's dictum, that the initial causes of conflict are to be sought in an insufficiency of supply to meet demand, honor as "an allegory of power permits the escalation of conflict outside and above the sphere of ecological friction, in a domain in which there are no material limits to restrict the magnitude of the prize."[26]

In feuding societies, honor and power are synonymous. A group's defense of its honor is actually its defense of its right to live in a given area and to exploit its birthright of natural resources. Through the exercise of physical violence, which causes fear and serves as a catalyst for construction of a network of alliances, each group ensures respect of its right to an equal place for itself in the social system through the process of feuding. The individual's defense of his own honor and that of his group provides an opportunity for self-aggrandizement and the acquisition of prestige. In an economically homogeneous society, a man's prestige is the only differentiating quality that he possesses from other members of the same society. In conditions of total scarcity, the translation of conflicts over materially limited goods into conflicts in which honor is the prize prevents extreme material scarcity from resulting in wide scale destruction.[27]

Italians, particularly Sicilians, constantly call upon the concepts of honor and shame in order to assess their own conduct and that of others. The *mafioso* as well as the *onorata società* embodies a general philosophy of life around the concepts of honor and shame. Both emerged from abnormal periods of hardship in Italian history. Both, possessing a profound mistrust of the state, never invoke civil laws in private quarrels. However, due to these various historical conditions, different types of vengeance cultures have arisen. We may say, in fact, that the culture of vengeance in Sardinia is a more "normal" feuding culture, in the sense that the feuds tend to contribute to the equilibrium of the society, and to provide a truly "religious" (i.e. cultural) meaning to the lives of the Sardinians.

On the other hand, we view criminal organizations such as the Mafia, as an "abnormal" development of feuding or vengeance, in the sense that Marx would view capitalism as a gruesome distortion of social life. We will see in chapter 9, for example, that the Mafia is, in fact, a prime example of the monopolization of honor. It accumulates honor and distributes it in a highly objectified form, rarely losing sight of the possibility of accumulating honor along with real capital. We can see how this "abnormal" development of vengeance can arise out of the special way in which feuding operates.

Feuding as Social Control

Feud often establishes relationships between hostile groups so that survival can be procured. This is achieved only in the absence of conditions conducive to a respected centralized authority and through the only means available—violence. Violence creates a balance of power as well as an internal hierarchy dominated by prestige, honor, and manliness. As a social system in its own right, feud operates successfully to control the relations between groups and coerce conformity to norms. Violence, being an integral part of the system, is the only instrument of social control; it is also a means of communication for the expression of temporary relations of dominance and submission. Thus, where scarcity reigns, feud and violence become synonymous with society and institution.

Given a continuing existence of conditions of scarcity, feud will be interminable, for it is the glue that is the "cohesive force" of a society.[28] As Black-Michaud states, "the evidence supporting the contention that feud is interminable survives and continues down the generations until physical distance or extermination bring about a permanent cessation of hostilities.[29] Feud often expresses and tests the varying quality of relationships between groups over interminable periods of time. It is often activated with the express purpose of testing stability of an existing relationship. There are many devices utilized to resuscitate feud from one generation to the next. Many preliterate societies have created a number of crude devices that serve to record the events of feud and to awaken successive generations to take vengeance for their ancestors.

In Somaliland, Southern Greece, Albania, and Corsica, it is the custom to improvise funerary dirges to incite the victim's dependents and close kin to wash the stain of blood from their house by spilling the blood of the killer or his near agnates. These dirges are remembered by the kin of the victim over whose bier they were sung, and are often repeated by community women for years after the event. This practice instills into the male heirs of the deceased, who may have been infants at the time of the killing, the necessity to carry out vengeance when they are old enough to bear arms.

Called *voceru, bucerata,* or *ballata* in Corsica,[30] and *kama* in Southern Greece[31], these improvisations are taken up by the people and occupy a position of importance in the repertory of local folk poetry. Busquet reports that the opprobrium suffered by a man who did not take vengeance after powerful provocation was so unendurable that the man would be forced to become a recluse out of shame. Albanians ostracize fellow tribesmen who have not bathed their honor in the blood of the killer of their kinsmen. A man was often reminded of his duty to vengeance by a glass of "rakia" that was passed to him in public from behind. If this tacit accusation of cowardice was ignored and no killing resulted, the man who had not avenged his own kinsmen was shunned by the society at large. We see here, the construction of an entire "superstructure," as Marx would call it, that buttresses and supports the social organization of feuding through the creation of a culture of beliefs, codes, and folk literature that supports the violence of feuding and above all, guarantees the continuation and expansion of the vengeance "market" feeding off past deeds, and projecting them onto individuals as yet unborn.

Vengeance and the Continuity of Feuding

At first, it would seem that each killing is only an isolated act perpetrated in revenge for the one that immediately preceded it. Yet by Peters's and Black-Michaud's definition, feuds are interminable. Each homicide inexorably leads to a sequence of hostilities. To understand the concept of interminability, it would perhaps be easier if we spoke of the original homicide as a "debt" and vengeance as the "redemption of the debt." Superiority can often be judged by the type of debt incurred. For example, the extension of credit for compensation to a killer rather than recourse to physical reprisal is tantamount to acknowledgment of his provisional superiority.

The idea that "debt" is the lubricant that keeps social relationships moving is not new to social anthropology. Arensberg described the ties between peasant farmers and shopkeepers in rural Ireland as a credit system in which "the debt the farmer owes, like the fortune he gives in marriage, is a tangible monetary symbol of alliance and mutual obligation."[32] Similarly, in feuding societies, if homicide inaugurates a relationship, the debt keeps it going. Peters goes so far as to state that all social relations are expressed in terms of the bond that ties the debtor to the creditor and vice versa.[33] The fact that debts are constantly left outstanding and there is always an absence of conclusion is reported in the literature of Albania, Egypt, Corsica, and Texas where feuds raged for the whole of the nineteenth century.[34]

We know that transactions by the exchange of goods and services contribute to the cohesion of societies, especially those at the level of subsistence economics.[35] Transactions in homicide and blood supplement the paucity of material wealth and provide a means of differentiating individuals and groups. This transaction is an unending process whereby the satisfaction of debts simultaneously creates new ones. Feud is thus an eternal relationship between groups who, by the manipulation of debt, endeavor to swing the pendulum of political dominance in their favor.

The constant antagonism between clans, which is a normal state of affairs, is disturbed with the accumulation of wealth, resulting in the production of inequality and class differentiation in the classic Marxist sense. In this case, the community as a whole tends to polarize, and under such conditions produces a large number of outlaws who express the collective needs of the group itself. Such outlaws are the topic of our next chapter: some of them have become America's heroes.

Notes

1. Henner Hess, *Mafia and Mafiosi: The Structure of Power*, trans. Edward Osers (Lexington, Mass: Lexington, 1970), p. 94.

2. Jacob Black-Michaud, *Cohesive Force: Feud in the Mediterranean and the Middle East* (Oxford: Basil Blackwell, 1975), p. 160.

3. Ibid., p. 160.

4. Ibid., p. 172.

5. Lewis Coser, *The Function of Social Conflict* (London: Routledge and Kegan Paul, 1956), p. 8.

6. Black-Michaud, *Cohesive Force*, p. 162.

7. The most well known of these are those of Albania: M. E. Durham, *High Albania* (London: Edward Arnold, 1909); idem, *Some Tribal Laws, Origins and Customs of the Balkans* (London: George Allen and Unwin, 1912); Margaret Hasluck, *The Unwritten Law of Albania*, eds. J. H. Hutton and Mrs. J. Anderson (Cambridge: Cambridge University Press, 1954). Calabria, Sicily, Corsica, and Sardinia: P. Marongiu, *Teoria e storia del banditismo sociale in Sardegna*, (Cagliari: Edizioni della Torre, 1981); E. Hobsbawn, *Primitive Rebels* (New York: Norton Library, 1959); J. Busquet, *Le Droit de la Vendetta et les Paci Corses* (Paris: Pedone, 1920), Turkey: J. K. Campbell, "The kindred in a greek mountain community," in Pitt-Rivers, ed., *Honor, Family and Patronage* (Oxford: Clarendon Press, 1964), pp. 73–96. The Middle East: Emyrs L. Peters, *The Sociology of the Bedouin of Cyrenaica*, Ph.D. dissertation, Oxford University, 1951.

8. Black-Michaud, *Cohesive Force*, p. 162.

9. Julian Pitt-River, in J. G. Perestiany, *Honor and Shame* (Chicago: University of Chicago Press, 1966), p. 25.

10. It is necessary to understand that Peters' study was based only on the Cyrenaican Bedouin, whose feuds are only confined to relations between groups at the same level of segmentation. This is why he placed so much emphasis upon equality among agnates.

11. Pitt-River, p. 25.

12. Ibid.

13. Karl Marx, *Capital,* trans. Ben Fowkes (New York: Vintage, 1977), vol. 1, chaps. 1–7.

14. "Circulation sweats money from every pore." *Capital*, p. 208.

15. This point is perhaps gratuitous, but one can see that this approach is opposed to Marxist theory, which holds that cultural attributes of a society (i.e. the superstructure) are a product of false consciousness that fails to attend to the basic economic inequalities in a society. The consciousness in feuding societies may be "false" (in the sense that it is a mental construction of men), but it certainly is not produced by economic inequality.

16. This difficulty has a long history. See Graeme Newman, *Just and Painful* with regard to reflected punishments.

17. This attribute of vengeance also explains why feuds are mostly interminable.

18. Black-Michaud, *Cohesive Force*, p. 193.

19. Ibid., p. 181.

20. Ibid., p. 178.

21. Of course, one may argue, and rightfully so, that honor plays an integral role among the aristocracy, where there does not exist a scarcity of resources. There are two replies to this argument: (1) Monarchs are under constant threat of treason and usurpation by other powers. Indeed, we know the special problems of princes as we have seen in the first three chapters of this book. (2) Ecological scarcity, although not being a present variable in the existence of an honor hierarchy, is still the origin of it.

22. Black-Michaud, *Cohesive Force*, p. 162.

23. That is, a truly good deed, should not expect repayment.

24. Henner Hess, *Mafia and Mafiosi: The Structure of Power*, trans. Edward Osers (Lexington, Mass: Lexington, 1970), p. 60.

25. Ibid., p. 94.

26. Ibid., p. 14. Honor may also serve as a pretext for conflict in the competition for control of natural resources. See E. J. Hobsbawm, *Primitive Rebels* (New York: W. W. Norton, 1959), p. 49. In Albania, for example, the question of honor is frequently invoked as a cause for hostilities. The conflict then provides a symbolic representation of the struggle for political dominance in those situations where conflicts for a material prize could imperil the very fabric of society. Evaluations of honor and its acceptance as a permissible excuse for armed confrontation creates "a symbolic arena for political strife in which prestige accruing from the successful outcome of a series of individual encounters can be accumulated to supply the bases of moral stratification despite a close adherence to the economic principle of a fair share for all." Hobsbawn, p. 50.

28. Richard Thurnwald, "Blood Vengeance Feud," in *Encyclopaedia of Social Sciences* 2: 598–99.

29. Black-Michaud, *Cohesive Force*, p. 74.

30. Busquet, *Le Droit a la Vendetta*.

31. Campbell, "The Kindred in a Greek Mountain Community."

32. Conrad Arensburg, *The Irish Countryman: An Informal History of the Underworld* (New York: Macmillan, 1937).

33. Peters, p. 350.

34. Sonnichsen, *Great Feuds of Texas* (New York: Devon-Adair, 1962) p. 372.

35. See Malinowski, *Crime and Custom in Savage Society* (Totowa, N.J.: Littlefield Adams & Co., 1964).

8

Vengeance as Protest: Jesse James and the Bandit Legend

It was as though three bandits had come to us from the storied Odenwald, with the halo of medieval chivalry upon their garments and shown us how the things were done that poets sing of.
—Major Edwards of the *Kansas City Times*, describing a bank robbery by the James gang in 1872.

"Come on Baker, if you are stinking for a fight; you never killed a man that you did not shoot in the back. Come and fight a man that's looking at you."
—Billy the Kid when he switched sides in the Lincoln County War, 1876.

Feuding in Texas

IN MOST STATES OF AMERICA, a man has to retreat as far back as he can before attempting to kill an attacker, whereas in Texas he can "stand his ground."[2] The traditional Texan code demands immediate and active response to an insult.

You can tell where a man is from the way he acts when you call him a liar. If he is from Texas he shoots you or knocks you down. If he is from Ohio he waves his fists and shouts, "And you're another?" If he is from New England he spits on a grasshopper and remarks calmly, "Well, you can't prove it."[3]

103

The violent response of Texans to afronts to their honor has often been taken as a sign of Texas lawlessness. This lawlessness, while often violent, originated in a period of Texas history that was fraught with chaos. This was during the Civil War and Reconstruction periods. Between 1868 and 1870, more than 900 (and possibly as many as 1,500) feud-related murders took place.[4]

William Sonnichsen, in his review of ten well-known Texas feuds, argues that the feud is not evidence of lawlessness, but rather is a reasonable substitute for legal redress when written law either has not yet arrived to the area or where legal remedies are not embraced because of a disorganized situation.[5] Feud occurs not among "the unrestrained, but among highly conservative people who cling to ancient folkways."[6] According to one Early American historian, vigilante committees (often the official representatives of feuding factions) are actually the expression of a highly developed belief in America of the "right of the governed at all times to instant and arbitrary control of the government."[7] The committee aims to "assist the law and to accomplish its purpose, even if it means resorting to unlawful means. The vigilante principle therefore does not spring from disrespect for law."[8] As we have suggested previously, vengeance can work well as a deterrent. A man, knowing that his death or that of his brothers would be a certainty, thinks twice before killing. In feuding Texas, the readiness of every citizen to right his own wrong helped intensify this maintenance of order through the fear of violence. Thus, where a formalized legal system did not exist, feud originated not with a sense of lawlessness, but rather with the need for order. The threat of feud provided the greatest deterrent to crime because of the rapidity and certainty of retaliation.

The usual hierarchical system of honor and shame developed in a special way. The quickest and most able to defend were regarded with the highest esteem, for they were the protectors. "The fastest gun in the West" became the most manly. The quest for honor often turned into an endless blood-bath. In fact, manliness seemed often to have overtaken the feud itself, with assassins changing sides regularly, according to who could pay the most.[9] Finally, the violence of battle itself—just as with Achilles—seems to have provided the only true satisfaction, expressed by Billy the Kid's threat to "die fighting with a revolver in each ear."[10]

The situation in the frontier was vastly different from that of feuds in other areas of Europe. There was not a situation of total scarcity. Rather, there was a vast country replete with natural resources—gold, land, and oil. Feuds over land rights, between cattlemen and farmers, and cattlemen and oilmen, were clearly feuds over the monopolization of material wealth. Assassins were employed by each faction, which, one suspects, had no consideration for "honor and shame," but rather was concerned with the acquisition of vast resources, or at least the defense of what it already had. We need only consider the "invasion" of Montana by the cattlemen of Texas to understand this, even though both sides claimed honor as justification for their violence. Furthermore, it is not altogether clear whether the forms of these "wars" were those of the more classic feuding cultures discussed in previous chapters, or those in which the balance of power had been subverted, as with the Mafia.[11]

Vigilante violence was also rampant at the time. This type of violence is a special "self-help" form of the feud; it is clear that it falls within the idea of "self-help" to ensure that "justice" is done.[12] Vengeance is clearly an important element of vigilante violence, but it must surely be clear that, according to our previous analysis, this collective form of vengeance is by far the most primitive, since there is no cultural code attached to it. However, even here it would be wrong to conclude that the cause of vigilantes is in and of itself "wrong." For example, the viglantes' pursuit and execution of the infamous, and by all accounts bloody murderer (and sheriff) Henry Plummer, would seem, given the inadequacy of established judicial procedures, to be in large part defensible.[13]

One final aspect of the Texas feuding period is worth noting, because it is virtually universal in other feuding cultures. Because of the strong reliance on local, self-help organizations to maintain order, the intervention from a "foreign" (i.e. any person or organization outside Texas, especially the East) was viewed with suspicion. This was especially so during and after the Civil War, which in Texas had as much to do with the autonomy of the state as with slavery. Furthermore, the U.S.

Government had imposed heavy taxes to pay for the war that was waged on southern and northern soil, and this was deeply resented.[14] The Texas constitution, which makes the legislative branch of government far more powerful than the executive or judicial branches, reflects the suspicion and fears of central government that dates back at least to Reconstruction (1865–1877).

In sum, we can see that the particular historical, geographical, and social conditions of the frontier produced feuding that was quite different in form from that of the feuding cultures of Europe and the Middle East. In our research, we have not been able to uncover any extensive material concerning detailed codes of conduct such as those of Mediterranean feuding societies. We have found only a few expressed principles—such as "stand one's ground," or "protect one's honor." In this sense, the "wild west" appears to have been lawless in the true sense of the word.

But the fact of the matter is that there was no clear code of honor because the feuds were carried on for material gain, and because those who abided by any code of honor, were *individuals* whose honor and manliness were, in a sense, appropriated by the various factions. Perhaps we see more strongly in American history, the clash between the ideal of rugged individualism, which militated against the essentially collective social organization of feuding. Unlike many Mediterranean societies with long feuding histories, the feuding of the wild west is truly past. There are no significant pockets of feuding left in the United States. Feuds live on now, not in reality, but in movies, books, television, comic strips, and in certain exterior aspects of Texas lifestyles. One need only note the popularity of weapons and their public display in Texas as a clear feature of the acceptance of the trappings of violence— the memorabilia of feuds gone by.[15]

These memorabilia have in different ways become part of the cultural mythology of the United States, and perhaps of much of western culture. We speak here of the legends of the wild west—the frontier mentality. These stories have only one theme, the one that we have argued is central to the origins of western culture—the preoccupation of the fight of the weak against the strong, the injustice of a world that is divided into the strong and the weak. From this deep cultural concern comes the yearning for the great, powerful, and all-good hero who protects the weak, and fights against the powerful. It is significant that this yearning for a hero, essentially a lone hero, should come from the United States where individualism is raised to the level of high honor.

The centrality of violence to this frontier mentality is undeniable. So also is the ambivalence concerning the righteous or evil nature of such individual heroes. We know why there is such ambivalence: it has to do with the use of violence, the impossibility to truly justify its use in the name of justice, since it is also the behavior of those who are condemned. We saw this problem clearly in Orestes and in Hamlet. And we can see it today in the apparently paradoxical view of the criminal as hero.

The Criminal as Hero

A number of scholars have tried to explain why many societies of east and west treat certain criminals as heroes, to the extent that their criminality is denied, and often justified as social protest.[16] With the exception of Eric Hobsbaum's classic work on social bandits, there has been a tendency to treat all such criminal heroes as the same, along with the common observation that their literary representation is vastly different from their actual deeds. Such characters as Jesse James, Billy the Kid, Jack Henry Abbott, and Gary Gilmore have been lumped together.[17] Their only similarity, however, is that, through the process of oral history, literature, and the media, these criminals have been ascribed certain attributes and motives. Depending on how close they are to us in history, and on the actual deeds that they perpetrated, the extent to which the ascription of these romantic characteristics "sticks," differs considerably. The recent attempts to romanticize the lives of Jack Henry Abbott[18] and Gary Gilmore[19] have been largely unsuccessful. That is to say, their criminal exploits have not been transformed into chivalrous acts. Furthermore, they were not leaders of bandit gangs. Rather, they were solitary criminals. The situation is much different with the heroes of the wild west, those whom we call "outlaws" rather than criminals—though they may have committed many crimes. Some of them were "loners," but most were leaders of bandit gangs.

In this chapter, we will examine the attribution of mythical characteristics to one of these outlaw-heroes, Jesse James. There have been many such outlaws in many different societies, such as Australia's Ned Kelly[20], England's Dick Turpin and Robin Hood[21], Mexico's Pancho Villa[22] and Zapata[23], Brazil's Antonio Silvino[24], Manolas the pirate of Greece[25], Algeria's Messaoud Ben Zelmat[26], and Nayan of Malaysia[27]. They have also appeared in many different historical periods.[28] These outlaws have been described by Eric Hobsbawm in his extensive work on social banditry as

> relatively small groups of men living on the margins of peasant society, and whose activities are considered criminal by the prevailing official power-structure and value-system, but not . . . by the peasantry.[20]

Hobsbawm has also described these bandits as "primitive rebels," a characterization that has come under considerable attack from Marxist writers who insist that these social bandits are not "primitive," but genuine revolutionaries produced by particular economic forces.[30] However, Hobsbawm, in spite of his critics, has addressed the more interesting questions: (1) what is the content and meaning of the attributes that society ascribes to these outlaw heroes, and (2) if their function is essentially social, why does the support that develops for them seem to focus so much on the individual personalities of a few? In order to answer these questions let us look closely at the history of Jesse James.

The Story of Jesse James

Jesse James was born near Kearny, Missouri on September 5, 1847. According to William Settle,[31] possibly the most reliable historian of the James gang and other bandits of the time, Jesse James was born of a preacher father who became a reasonably prosperous landholder with 275 acres. The family owned seven slaves and a number of sheep and livestock. One day his father suddenly left to go west in search of gold; he died there a year later. Jesse's mother married twice thereafter, her last husband being a certain Dr. Samuel.

Little is known of the James brothers' boyhood. Many attempts have been made to reconstruct it to account for later exploits, such as claims that they delighted in cutting off dogs' tails or torturing animals. There is no actual corroboration of these stories. Rather, the consensus of opinion seems to be that their boyhood was not especially different from that of other boys of those same turbulent times.

Certainly, the violent period in American history in which the James boys grew up must have had an impact on them. The bloody marauding of guerilla bands several years prior to the outbreak of the Civil War, and the apparent inability of many Confederate soldiers to settle down after the war must have had an important effect on the lives of all boys at the time. It is not clear, however, why the James boys should have become much more violent than the majority of boys. It is clear, of course, that the events surrounding the Civil War can explain why a much larger number of young men fell into banditry, since it seems to have been so much a part of life. But the puzzle—so familiar to criminologists—still remains as to why particular individuals choose a violent way of life, and the majority, in times that are highly conducive to it, do not.

Eric Hobsbawm[32] has provided a possible solution to this puzzle. He suggests that, of all the famous bandits he has been able to review, there was always a precipitating incident early in their lives, commonly during the most "crime prone" age, (according to criminologists, which is late adolescence from 16 to 24 years of age).[33] This precipitating incident usually, if not always, conforms to the following formula. The hero leads a quiet, unexceptional childhood amidst the chaos and repression of an authoritarian or dictatorial foe who usually exists outside the local community in which the hero lives. He often leads a life close to the earth, almost always a rural life. He goes about his business, not becoming involved in violence— even shunning it. But fate will not leave him be. The foreign foe intrudes into his family life. Either he is accused of acting against the "established law" (which is seen by the local community as arbitrarily imposed upon them, and therefore unjust), or the accusation is made against innocent family members.

Sooner or later, the established order (militia men, special police etc.) falls upon them, and commits terrible atrocities in order to get from them information about bandit activities. A family member may be killed, raped, or tortured, the hero himself falsely accused and beaten. In any event, under such extreme provocation, the hero is "forced into" banditry, and henceforth his terrible blood-thirstiness is "justified" on the basis of this early, provocative act. His entire bandit life is seen and interpreted as a lifestyle motivated (and justified by) the need to avenge the injustices done his family.

Jesse James is no exception to this pattern. While it is always difficult to separate fact from fiction as far as the James story is concerned, there is little doubt that there was, in fact, one early incident (and probably other lesser ones) that provided the impetus for Jesse and his brother Frank to join up with one of the marauding guerilla bands that roamed the countryside. The guerilla bands at the time claimed a vague ideological purpose—to resist the Northerners' intrusion into Missouri, especially their attempt to abolish slavery. But we know that the bands did not manage to focus their violence on Northerners alone, but from time to time ravaged, apparently at will, settlers in many parts of Missouri and Kansas.

It would appear that Frank James (the elder of the two) was the first to join a band in 1863 when he rode with Quantrill's guerillas and participated in the Lawrence massacre in which they killed in cold blood some 150 men and boys. Some time in 1864, Jesse James, at the age of 17, joined one of the most bloodthirsty gangs of the time, led by Bill Anderson. Story has it that Jesse's family had been roughed up by the militia men. His stepfather, Dr. Samuel, had been half hanged in order to get information from him about local bandits, his mother "abused," and he himself lashed severely in the fields where he was ploughing. So it was that he rode with Anderson and his gang on August 12 and 13, 1864 on the Centralia massacre. Again, many men and boys were killed in cold blood. It was here that Jesse James received two of the severe wounds that became part of his legend. The severe injury to the side, it was said, would have killed any other man, but Jesse miraculously survived it. And he lost the tip of the middle finger of his left hand—an injury that would make it possible to identify his body when he was finally killed.

From this time on, Frank and Jesse James were involved in many bank and train robberies, and they became famous for their daring. In one foray, they robbed a bank while the entire town's population was in church, then went into the church to inform the townspeople that their bank had been robbed. The churchgoers were reluctant to believe that the James gang was telling the truth, and by the time they found out, the gang was far away.

The local press glorified their exploits, and they enjoyed much popular support. Local and state elections were even fought on the platform of pro and con banditry. Attempts were made to obtain amnesty for the James boys and others of their gang. However, by 1873, the governor of Missouri, under considerable pressure to remove the slur of "uncivilized and primitive," as his state was often described by the eastern press, attempted to have the Pinkerton men, who had been very effective in capturing and solving other serious crimes, try to capture the James boys. This resulted in the killing of four Pinkerton men in circumstances that were "unexplained." Worse still, these efforts resulted in events that simply added to the richness of the Jesse James legend. In 1873, two Pinkerton men threw a fire bomb into the James's house. Dr. Samuel and his wife tried to push it into the fireplace, but it exploded. Their eight-year-old son (Jesse's half brother) was killed, and Jesse's mother had her arm blown off. The James boys were not captured.

This event created an outcry among the people and the journalists who had been doing their best to embellish the James legend. Another attempt was made to pass legislation granting amnesty to the James boys and others in their gang. It was not passed. Instead, the governor had secretly made available a reward of $20,000 for the capture of Jesse and Frank James, "Dead or Alive."

Jesse lived under the name of Frank Howard in a quiet town, and took into his house two young boys who were planning to ride with him on his next bank robbery. The younger of these boys, Robert Ford, who had not yet ridden with Jesse, waited until he had Jesse's confidence. One morning, Jesse stepped up on a chair to straigthen a picture. Bob Ford drew his pistol and shot Jesse in the back of the head. Jesse James fell down dead. It was April 3, 1882.

Many people who had known Jesse were enlisted to provide positive identification that it really was Jesse James. Over the years, there had been many reports that he was dead, but Jesse had kept showing up. So it was very important to establish his death once and for all. This time he was identified by the well known scars on his body. Yet there were many who refused and continued to refuse to believe that Jesse James was dead. It has been common since then for people to claim that they were Jesse James—the most recent and famous being Frank Dalton in 1950.[34]

Thus died the hero and avenger. His brother Frank lived to an old age, having been found not guilty in two widely publicized trials. The legend has been preserved in movies, novels, and in the well-known ballad of Jesse James, which tells of his robbing from the rich and giving to the poor. The chorus laments that he was shot by "a dirty little coward."

Jesse James: Social Bandit or Culture Hero?

In his romantic image, Jesse James represents a diffuse sense of injustice, a sense that transcends the individual and family, to represent a social collective, usually a small community, most often the poor. We must be clear, however, that his original motive (and possibly his real one) was to avenge the injustice done to his family. But the *cultural function* (that is, the meaning) of his actions was to express the injustice done to *all* families who saw themselves unjustly treated by a "foreign" force. This attribution of a broader social motivation is known as the Robin Hood ethic.

The best sources are unable to confirm the actual existence of Robin Hood,[35] but we are all well acquainted with the stories of the unjust oppression of the peasant people by the Sheriff of Nottingham, and the kindliness of Robin to the poor. His entire lifestyle and that of his "merry band" was devoted to maintaining the "balance of power" between the peasants and the Sheriff. And always in the background there was the specter of a distant and arbitrary king who supported the unjust order that the Sheriff of Nottingham so enthusiastically implemented. Of course, Robin Hood could appeal to the "true king," good King Richard, to justify his exploits and crimes against the established order.[36]

A similar story line is found in the legend of Jesse James:[37]

> Jesse and his gang, in a daring raid, rob a bank. They are hotly pursued by the local posse. They manage to elude their pursuers and, hot and tired, come across a small homestead inhabited by a poor, lonely widow. Her husband has usually been killed by militiamen. She invites Jesse and his gang in to eat and rest, and water their horses. While she is taking care of them, she tells her story. It turns out that she is awaiting the arrival, any minute, of the bank manager, who is

about to foreclose on her farm because she cannot pay her loan. She rings her hands in grief.

Not to worry! Jesse produces the loot he has taken from the bank and gives her the entire amount needed to pay off the mortgage. They hear the bank manager approaching, and leave quickly. The bank manager, relishing the thought of assuming ownership of the farm, arrives, showing no mercy for the poor old widow. But to his amazement, she pays him the whole amount and he has no choice but to turn over the deed of ownership. He leaves very puzzled.

We can guess what happens next. Jesse and his gang lie in wait for this money hungry bank man. They hold him up and retrieve their money . . . and justice has been done! The balance, always unfairly tilted toward the rich, is once again moved a little more to the poor.

It is likely that Robin Hood never existed at all.[38] Similarly, while we know that Jesse James did in fact exist, and that he did indeed perform many of the exploits people said he did, there is no evidence that he robbed from the rich and gave to the poor.[39] The legend of Jesse James was constructed both by the media of the time, and by embellishments added through the process of oral history.

Therefore, we must conclude that James and his bandit gang were not social bandits in the Marxist sense (as many of Hobsbawm's critics have argued) since they performed no *political* function. That is to say, they were not rebelling against societal injustice, nor were they fighting for a social program that they believed in. And there is certainly no reason to claim that James and his gang fought on the basis of a "class consciousness" as one later interpreter of these bandits has insisted.[40] (It is, however, quite possible that other famous bandits *were* embarked on an ideological and revolutionary enterprise. Such a case might be made for Pancho Villa,[41] although some writers are of the opinion that Pancho Villa valued his violent way of life more than everything else.[42] He did indeed switch political sides with some agility.[43] It may certainly be argued that some peasant uprisings, often led by bandit heroes, had a clear ideological function—Castro's revolution in Cuba is perhaps the best example,[44] and it has been argued that the communist revolution in China was preceeded by extensive social banditry.)[45]

But none of the ancient heroes described in this book displayed the kindliness and care of a Robin Hood, nor were they interested in revolution. Indeed, the Greek heroes' main motivation seemed to be to take care of only one injustice—

their own individual oppression, without much care for others. Even in Hamlet, the care for the plight of others does not extend outside the immediate families of the protagonists. There is no generalized concern for others.

In sum, we argue that, while the vengeance of Jesse James is of a very primitive stage, it is at least one step ahead of the stage of individual responsibility (as in Hamlet). There is the beginning of vengeance on behalf of a vaguely defined, generalized other, although the "other" is also limited to a small local community. This is the first stage in the idea of vengeance as a social responsibility, one that is not so clearly and narrowly defined as in feuding subcultures that support closed clans or families, and where the lines of who are the enemy are clearly drawn. But the fact remains that this elemental social step is not fulfilled by action: the deeds of the bandit gang are largely predatory, praying on rich and poor alike.

Our conclusion is that an ideal social function is ascribed to these actors and their deeds. In other words, their acts and lives are transformed into myth; they are given *cultural* meaning. Strictly speaking, Jesse James is not a social bandit. He is a culture hero.

Cultural Traits of the Bandit

1. *Basic motivation.* We have argued that the basic motivation of the mythical heroes was an elementary sense of injustice. The origin of this sense of injustice was an arbitrary act of oppression by the all powerful father against the sons: an act of terrible proportions, the attempt to eat them. With the James story, the act of oppression is no longer contained within the family but comes from a foreign source. And the rebellion is likewise directed outside the family rather than against the father within it. No doubt psychologists would like to show that Jesse's rebellion was somehow related to his treatment by his father, perhaps his having been deserted by his father who "went West." But there is really no necessity to embark on such speculation since we can look elsewhere for the source of his rebellion: the elementary sense of injustice precipitated by a ruthless, ilegitimate, and unjustified attack on him and his family.

Almost all of the literature on Jesse James tries to explain (and justify) his subsequent lifestyle totally in terms of this precipitating act. The elementary sense of injustice remains all pervasive. Can Jesse's bank robberies be reasonably characterized as acts of rebellion rather than criminal acts perpetrated for monetary gain? A number of contemporary east coast journalists were quite satisfied to call Jesse James a thug, and expressed exasperation at the apparent tolerance shown to him by the Missouri authorities.[46]

The fact is that the "rebellious" acts of Jesse James were, in themselves, doomed to failure if we take "success" to mean the overthrow of the established order. No matter how many violent acts he committed, how many banks he robbed, there was no way that he could restore the sense of equilibrium that is the driving force behind the elementary sense of injustice— that is, the equal exchange of one violent act for another, the switch from being the oppressed to the oppressor.

We have no way of knowing what James was thinking, or what he personally hoped to achieve each time he robbed a bank. Maybe he did it for the money. No matter. For, even if he could be shown never to have cared about injustice, one could still argue that it is more important that the mythical reconstruction of his acts does indeed promote this motivation. Thus, while Jesse's acts of "rebellion" were in themselves doomed to failure, the mythical reconstruction of his life is anything but that. The myth achieves what reality could not.

2. *God-like qualities.* The Greek gods were described as invincible, invulnerable, invisible, capable of tremendous destruction and violence, and vindictive. Achilles had tremendous strength, and was (except for his heel) invulnerable. Ulysses similarly was as cunning as a god, and by using this mental agility, he managed to extricate himself from many a sticky situation.

The myth of Jesse James portrays his god-like qualities. He committed the first bank robbery in the United States, and of the many later committed, there was constant conjecture as to whether or not the James boys were involved. Typically, a bank robbery would be committed in one town, and an interview with Jesse James would be published, purportedly conducted at the same time in another town. How could he be in two places at once? Only a god could manage such a feat.

Nor were the many posses ever able to track him down. He and his gang were able to "vanish into thin air." Of course, his

vanishing act was aided by local inhabitants who were prepared to hide him. But no matter. As far as the mythology is
concerned, he was more than human. Posses were simply no
match for him.[47]

Gods don't die either—and many thought that Jesse James
just couldn't die. He received two serious wounds to his chest
on various raids—and recovered miraculously, especially
from the second, which had damaged his lung, so that the
doctor pronounced his death inevitable. There were many
reports of his death, later to be proven false when he reap-
peared to rob yet another bank or train. When he was finally
killed, many refused to believe it.[48]

Perhaps his most startling god-like trait was his capacity to
commit violence. People who put up the slightest resistance to
him and his gang were quickly shot dead. In comparison to
other bandits, however, we could say that Jesse James was a
little less "terrible" in this regard. There was no ritual slaying
in the sense of leaving particular disfigurements on the bodies
as occurred in the vengeance cultures we have described in
the previous chapter. Rather, the killings by the James gang
appear to have been highly goal-oriented and pragmatic. The
more terrible and uncontrolled killings and destruction occurred before they had formed their gang, when they rode
with Anderson's guerilla bands. Guerilla skirmishes are more
similar to feuds in their operation. Perhaps this is what
separates Jesse James from other social bandits such as Zapata
and Pancho Villa; the latter wreaked tremendous destruction,
and they did so by raising guerilla bands that became virtual
armies. The James gang was very much a gang, with no lofty
guerilla role.

3. *Destroyed by treason.* In many of the stories we have told,
the hero or mythical god was betrayed by someone close to
him. This occurred with Cronos, Agamemnon, and Hamlet.
(We need hardly note, by the way, that the betrayal of Christ
also fits this model nicely). The same applied to Jesse James.[49]
It is especially significant that the traitor should have been
someone younger than Jesse, a fact that also fits into our
model. That it was not one of his family, however, is of some
interest to us, for it suggests once agains that the myth of Jesse
James represents an important developmental step in the
externalization of vengeance away from the family. The traitor

was a new member of his band and one who had gained his confidence. Jesse would have been wise to keep things in his family—yet we know from the stories and myths we have described so far that there lies equal or worse danger from within. Certainly, the cries of his mother at the inquiry concerning Jesse's death clearly displayed her view that one cannot trust anyone outside the family. If social bandits retained this view, it would, of course, not be possible for them to act as true social bandits, since they would be forced to fight for their family's welfare rather than for the welfare of a class or group that cut across family lines.

4. *Conflict.* We find here the most worrying feature of the Jesse James myth. As far as one can tell, Jesse James seems to have suffered little conflict about what he did. He robbed banks and trains. He wrote letters to Major Edward's paper claiming innocence (both in terms of, "he didn't do it," and if he did, it was entirely justified because he was merely robbing from the rich to give to the poor). It will be remembered that the Greek gods suffered no conflicts either. Rather, each god tended to represent a particular human trait, and the entire set of gods, it could be said, represented the array of human emotions and intellect. As the psychology of western man evolved, the god-men such as Achilles and Ulysses began to show a wider range of traits, although conflicts within their characters were still represented by fights that went on among the gods. Not until Hamlet do we find that these conflicts have been internalized. We argued, in our chapter on Hamlet, that this represented an important developmental step in the maturation of western man, and of vengeance in particular.

But in Jesse James we find no internal conflict—except the initial wavering as to whether he would take up violence. But even here, he is provided with such a clear provocation that conflict over such a decision seems hardly to arise. Instead, we must look elsewhere for conflict, and the logical place to look may be the gang itself. Here we find a particularly interesting set of circumstances. It is very well documented that the two James brothers were a contrast in personalities.[50] Jesse was the impetuous, youthful, outgoing, spotaneous personality of the two—the Dyonisian, if you will. But his brother Frank was very much the opposite. He was a quiet, withdrawn person, a morose personality, much older-looking with a full beard; he

was a cool planner, methodical and careful. (Perhaps this
explains why it is that it was Frank who survived to old age).
The contrasts in their personalities are startlingly evident, as
though the two brothers were each of two different gods. We
hesitate to suggest that this split, or failure to internalize these
basic psychological characteristics is symptomatic of a rever-
sion to an earlier stage in the development of vengeance.

5. *Obsessive.* The obsessive nature of the greek gods and
classical heroes is clear for all to see. They were driven by an
elementary sense of injustice and were unable to rest until this
sense was in some way "satisfied." The resolution of this
elementary sense of injustice became an obsession, in the
sense that it dominated everything the hero did. This observation clearly applies to all the heroes we have described from
Achilles to Hamlet. It applies also to Jesse James, who appeared to do little else than rob banks and trains, and between
robberies, after momentary satisfaction of the elementary
sense of injustice, retired to oblivion to plough his fields.

There could be no peace, however, for the robbing of an
occasional bank, while giving temporary satisfaction, could
not possibly, by itself, alter the basic social structure that
produces the haves and have nots. The only solution to this
problem is either to give up one's attempts altogether (as did
Frank James after Jesse was killed), or to raise one's sights
much higher, with the view to conducting a revolution. The
latter requires an ideological commitment, or at least an opera-
tional policy (which Jesse James seems not to have had, except
for that fed him through the media of Major Edwards), plus the
raising of a guerilla band, and subsequently an army. Again,
Jesse James made no such attempt. In contrast, Pancho Villa,
within the broader scope of his rebellious role, knew that he
must raise an army if he was to defeat his foes whom he
clearly saw in political terms.[51]

6. *Honor.* We saw previously that honor was the medium of
exchange in cultures of vengeance. As far as one can tell, there
was very little honor among the James gang and others like it.
They killed and maimed on whim. Their victims never had a
chance. This is in stark contrast to the imagery that was
developed around him. We need only see the descriptions of
him by Major Edwards, in his editorial titled "The Chivalry of
Crime" for the *Kansas City Times*, to see the process of

ascribing to Jesse the qualities of a gentleman and honorable man:[52]

> These men never go upon the highway in lonesome places to plunder the pilgrim. That they leave to the ignobler pack of jackals . . . a feat of stupendous nerve and fearlessness . . . becomes chivalric; poetic; superb.

And in a letter Major Edwards claimed was written by Jesse James himself:[53]

> What have we done to be hung for? It is true that I shot a little girl, though it was not intentional, and I am very sorry that the child was shot; and if the parents will give me their address . . . I will send them money to pay her doctor's bill.

The letter goes on to implore readers to rank him among the great "bold robbers," such as Alexander the Great and Julius Caesar. The dime novelists of the time indulged in similar constructions in an effort to create the image of the honorable and "just" outlaw, with a healthy mix of adventure, and manliness, of course.[54]

The ascription of honor to the hero bandit is an interesting attenuation of the transformation of vengeance into honor as we described in chapter 7. While in feuding societies honor assumes a place of central importance in the everyday lives of the individuals on each side of the feud, this is not the case with the avenging hero. Rather, the hero receives passive support of the local community, which does not live by this code. The local peasants are usually concerned with surviving. Marxists would say that they do not have a "consciousness of themselves as a class." Whatever the interpretation, one thing is certain: while they may hide the gang, or throw the authorities off the track when they chase the outlaw, they do not take up arms with him. Their support is passive, and they get in return a *representation* of their collective sense of injustice. Through Jesse James and other hero bandits, the bulk of the community "sees justice done." And we have seen that it is inevitable that violence will be used against injustice, but that its use must be filtered through the cultural transformation of vengeance. Honor and manliness therefore are the key attributes ascribed to the personalities of the hero bandits, for it is only through these traits that violence can be neutralized, and more importantly, its value as a defense against injustice can be readily apprehended.

Vengeance as Social Protest

As we have seen, Hobsbawm has called bandits like Jesse James "primitive rebels," by which he meant that they were a preliminary stage in rebelling against the social order, but did not represent a class as distinct from a small group, gang, or family. It would appear, however, that when a third party attempted to assert itself from places external to the local village or area, that these rebels often gravitated towards representing class concerns, and that, in fact, rebel gangs did join together to form the elementary structure of class interests.[55]

What interest could such figures as Jesse James represent? There were many possible class interests that could have been represented such as the landed against the landless, or slaves against the slave owners. But it must be said, that from a Marxist perspective, the "objective conditions" for revolution were not present in the form of a clear economic conflict between the proletariat and the owners of production, nor was there a discernible "class consciousness" among the ranks of the landless. Indeed, it was very often those who owned land who were inclined to support the James gang, simply because they represented to them values they cherished, such as the retention of slaves, and the strong and violent preservation of individual rights.

Of course, it does not make much sense to talk about a proletariat in the wild west, since Marx had in mind an industrial proletariat, and there was very little industry, save the railroad, in the West. It makes more sense, therefore, to try to analyze the Jesse James phenomenon as an earlier, developmental stage in the growth of "class consciousness," or, to put it another way, as a precursor to—or perhaps substitute for—organized rebellion.

Throughout this book we have focused heavily on the oppression by the powerful of the weak. We are able to see, so far, in all the stories of the heroes that they often face impossible odds, in fact, almost always so. It is only through superhuman acts that they are able to overcome them. We may interpret this phenomenon as an expression of the helplessness of the downtrodden. They are, by definition, too weak to do anything about their condition. They are able, therefore, to gain some measure of hope, by looking towards the super-leader who, although he is thought of as a leader, they do not follow in an active sense but can support passively. That is, to support the hero actively is generally to ask too much of these ordinary people who have families, children, homes, and jobs to care for. They have too much at stake to openly support these heroes. This is surely why the members of these bandit gangs are composed of young men who are unmarried and without families, or who have lost their families in some tragedy. The people support these outlaws passively, therefore, by hiding them, feeding them, and misdirecting law enforcement officials concerning their whereabouts. Most of them do not actively take up arms.

The irony is that, depending upon the particular social, political, and historical conditions, the local inhabitants can pay a high price for this passive support. That same kind of passive support can be subverted and appropriated by the most ruthless brokers of honor and vengeance: the Mafia and its many counterparts throughout the world.

Notes

1. Pat F. Garrett, *The Life of Billy the Kid* (New York: Leisure Books, n.d.) originally published in 1882 by New Mexican Printing and Publishing Company. The Lincoln County war raged for several years between the large cattle herders whose herds of 80,000 head ranged up and down Texas, against a consortium of small cattle owners who complained that their herds were destroyed by the large owners.

2. *Horbach v. State*, Texas Supreme Court Reports XLIII, 1883, pp. 242–61; *Brown v. U.S.*, 256 U.S. 335, 41 S. Ct. 501, 65 L. ed 161, 18 A. L. R. 1276, decided by Justice Holmean, 1921.

3. William Sonnichsen, *Ten Texas Feuds* (Albuquerque: University of New Mexico Press, 1957), pp 1–7.

4. R. N. Richardson, *Texas, the Lone Star State* (New York: Prentice Hall, 1943).

5. Ibid.

6. C. L. Sonnichsen, *The Story of the Great Feuds of Texas* (New York: Devon-Adair, 1962), p. 371.

7. George Bancroft, *History of the United States* (Boston: Little Brown, 1866).

8. Ibid.

9. Billy the Kid switched sides, even though it meant fighting against his lifelong friend, Jesse Evans.

10. Garrett, *Billy the Kid*, p. 142.

11. See A. S. Mercer's classic, *The Banditti of the Plains* (Norman: University of Oklahoma Press). The cattlemen hired assassins to systemati-

cally kill their opponents. However, that this was a battle of words as well as guns is attested to by the fact that almost all copies of Mercer's book were destroyed and biased newspaper articles were planted in the local and national press.

12. Donald Black, "Crime as Social Control," *American Sociological Review*, 48 (February, 1984): pp. 34–45.

13. T. J. Dimsdale, *The Vigilantes of Montana* (Norman: University of Oklahoma Press, 1954).

14. William Sonnichsen, *The Great Feuds*.

15. It is probably true that there are still some isolated pockets of feuding in the south, remnants perhaps of the famous feuds such as the Peacock Feud, the Hovell-Higgins feud, the Jaybird-Woodpecker feud, the Brooch Wall Feud, and the Hatfield-McCoy feud. See O. K. Rice, *The Hatfields and the McCoys* (Lexington: University of Kentucky Press, 1978); V. C. Jones, *The Hatfields and the McCoys* (Chapel Hill: University of North Carolina Press, 1948).

16. See P. F. M. Angiolillo, *The Criminal as Hero* (Lawrence, Kansas: The Regents Press of Kansas, 1979); Teresa G. Phelps, "The Criminal as Hero in American Fiction," *Wisconsin Law Review*, 6(1983): 1427–1454, Paul G. Kooistra, *American Robin Hoods: The Criminal as Social Hero*, Ph.D. dissertation, University of Virginia, 1982.

17. Phelps, *The Criminal as Hero* pp. 1427–1454.

18. Abbott was released after a campaign by Norman Mailer and other literary figures. He committed another murder two weeks after his release. See Jack Henry Abbott, *In the Belly of the Beast* (New York: Vintage, 1982). Phelps argues persuasively that Abbott was not as "talented" as Mailer and others claimed: Phelps, *The Criminal as Hero* pp. 1427–1454.

19. N. Mailer, *The Executioner's Song* (New York: Warner, 1979).

20. Pat O'Malley, "Class Conflict, Land and Social Banditry: Bushranging in 19th Century Australia," *Social Problems*, 26 (Feb. 1979): 271–83.

21. Kent Steckmesser, *The Western Hero in History and Legend* (Norman: University of Oklahoma Press, 1965).

22. Oren Arnold, *The Mexican Centaur: An Intimate Biography of Pancho Villa* (Tuscaloosa, Alabama: Portals, 1979).

23. Peter E. Newell, *Zapata of Mexico* (Sanday, Orkney, England: Cien Fuegos, 1979).

24. Linda Lewing, "Oral Tradition and Elite Myth: The Legend of Antonio Silvino in Brazilian Popular Culture," *Journal of Latin American Lore*, vol. 5 no. 2(1979): 157–204.

25. Pierre B. Gravel, "A Legend in the Making: Manolas the Pirate," Journal of Folklore Institute, vol. 15 no. 3(1978): 253–62.

26. Joan Dejeux, "Un Bandit d'Honneur l'Aures, de 1917a 1921," *Revue de l'Occident Musulman et de la Méditerranée* 26(1978): 35–54.

27. Cheah Boon King, "Social Banditry and Rural Crime in North Kedah, 1909–1929," *Journal of the Malaysian Branch of the Royal Asiatic Society* 54, 2(1981): 98–130.

28. See Hobsbawm, *Primitive Rebels* and *Bandits*; Thomas L. Engelen, "De Bokherijders," *Spiegel Hist.* 14, 3(1979): 135–141; Stencke, Wolfgang, "Schinderhannes and Co: Crime and Bandits in the 18th and 19th Centuries," *Frankfurter Heft*, 35, 3(1980): 47–54.

29. E. J. Hobsbawm, "Social Banditry," In H. W. Landsberger, ed., *Rural Protest, Peasant Movements and Social Change* (London: Macmillan, 1974), p. 143.

30. See for example, Pat O'Malley, "Social Bandits, Modern Capitalism and the Traditional Peasantry," *Journal of Peasant Studies*, 6(1979): 489–501.

31. William Settle's *Jesse James was His Name* (Columbia: University of Missouri Press, 1966) of the many books written on Jesse James, is probably the most scholarly. At least the author has gone to great lengths to separate fact from fiction.

32. Hobsbawm, *Primitive Rebels*, also *I Banditi* (Torino: Einaudi, 1971), p. 38.

33. So far, this would also apply to Billy the Kid, although the imposition of a foreign "order" that unjustly intervened is more difficult to establish. See W. Noble Burns, *The Saga of Billy the Kid* (New York: Garden City, 1926).

34. People refused to believe that Billy the Kid was dead, even though Garrett (his slayer) was able to provide plenty of evidence that he had indeed shot him. This belief was fueled by the fact that no death certificate was filed. See Stephen Tatum, *Inventing Billy the Kid: Visions of the Outlaw in America* (Alberquerque: University of New Mexico Press, 1982).

35. K. Steckmesser, "Robin Hood and the American Outlaw," *Journal of American Folklore*, 79 (April-June 1966): 348–55.

36. Hobsbawm, *I Banditi*, p. 37. According to Hobsbawm, the "ideal figure" of the noble robber has nine features. Among them, we find that the bandit does not fight against the king or emperor as sources of justice, but rather against local bosses, priests, and other oppressors.

37. Larry C. Bradley, *Jesse James: The Making of a Legend* (Nevada, Missouri: Larren Publishers, 1980).

38. Settle, *Jesse James*, passim.

39. Settle, *Jesse James*, passim.

40. O'Malley, "Social Bandits, Modern Capitalism." This does not mean that class conflict did not exist. It is simply to argue that these bandits were not part of this conflict.

41. See M. L. Guzman, *The Memoirs of Pancho Villa*, (Austin: University of Texas Press, 1965).

42. E. Beltran, "Fantasia y Realidad de Pancho Villa," *Hist. Mexicana* 16, 1(1966): 71–84, argues that Villa was merely a self-seeking criminal, not a revolutionary.

43. Hobsbawm, *Bandits*, passim.

44. Works that generally take the view of banditry as a precursor to peasant uprising are: Allen Isaacman, "Social Banditry in Zimbabwe and Mozambique 1894–1907: An Expression of Early Peasant Protest," *Journal of South African Studies* 4, 1: 1–30; H. A. Garza, "Political Economy and Change: The Zapatista Agrarian Revolutionary Movement," *Rural Sociology* 44(1979): 2211–306; I. K. Vasdravelles, "Men of war in Macedonia during the Prerevolutionary Period," *Makedonika*, 7(1966–67): 31–76.

45. Phil Billingsley, "Banditism Bosses and Bare Sticks: Beneath the Surface of Local Control in Early Republican China," *Modern China*, 7, 3(1981): 235–88. See also Hobsbawm, *I Banditi*, p. 103.

46. Settle, *Jesse James*, passim.

47. "Since nobody tips off the police, the bandits are virtually invisible." Hobsbawm, *I Banditi*, pp. 45–46.

48. Ibid., p. 46.

49. "Jesse James, according to the myth, never robbed priests, widows, orphans or ex-confederates." Ibid., pp. 44–45.

50. Settle, *Jesse James*, passim.

51. Hobsbawm, *Bandits*, passim.

52. *Kansas City Times*, September 27, 1872.

53. *Kansas City Times*, October 15, 1874.

54. See John Cawelti, *The six-gun Mystique* (Bowling Green: Bowling Green University Press, 1975); Kooistra, *America's Robin Hoods*, pp. 67–144; Tatum, *Inventing Billy the Kid* demonstrates this process most effectively.

55. Pat O'Malley, "The Suppression of Social Banditry: Train Robbers in the U.S. Border States and Bushrangers in Australia, 1865–1905," *Crime and Social Justice* 16 (Fall 1981): 32–41.

9

Brokers of Vengeance:
The Mafia

But if you ask me, in passing, just to talk about life, and whether it is right to take away a man's life, I say: "You have first to see if he *is* a man."[1]

IT IS CLEAR THAT, for the mafioso Don Mariano who pronounced these words in an important part of the novel, *Il giorno della civetta* (The Day of the Owl), not all men are men, and consequently, "in the view of the mafiosi all lives do not have the same value,"[2] It is also clear that the elimination of those who are not, strictly speaking, men, in the sense that they are distant from the ideal model accepted by the Mafia mentality, is not considered a crime. Indeed, it is more often seen as a duty.

The Mafiosa Way

The Mafia has one *weltanschaung*, a peculiar mentality that was created and developed in particular historical circumstances, from which the various criminal organizations grew.[3] This mentality has become known as "mafiosa," a strict style of behavior governing interpersonal relationships within and outside the organization.

This style expresses a philosophy and system of goals to be

125

reached, and most of all, a strategy for reaching those goals. Since its first appearance and development in Sicily in the last century, we may also consider the Mafia an attenuated category of the "man of honor," who tries to achieve power and personal prestige, and then to maintain and expand his influence. The method by which he achieves these honorable goals, is through intimidation and threats of violence. In this cultural system, the importance of conquering and maintaining an honorific position has produced the idea of the Mafia as an "honored society."[4]

For a long time, when the Mafia mentality was just taking shape, to be a man of honor and to act as a mafioso were the same. Thus, it is not surprising that the word omertà itself, which indicates the rule of silence and solidarity with individuals who do not collaborate with the state, comes from the Sicilian dialect omu, which means man. This means that a real man, or in other words, an honored man, would never break this rule, under the penalty of the loss of honor itself. The rule of omertà, which is also derived from the need for the self-defense of the subcultural system against external threats, is expressed in a number of proverbs and popular sayings[5]

> The man who is a real man, reveals nothing, not even at the point of a knife
>
> The man who talks a lot doesn't say anything, the man who doesn't talk at all is wise.
>
> Once upon a time Speaking and Eating asked King Soloman which of them should dominate man's mouth, and Soloman decided that Eating should dominate man's mouth and not Speaking, for fear that Speaking might become man's downfall. Ever since, man has been the more successful the less he speaks.
>
> The priest covers the chalice and we must cover one another.

The same rule is not only an expression of subcultural needs, but seems to be connected to a broader idea of man according to which one must achieve and maintain honor using only one's own individual resources.[6] At least in the beginning, the mafioso was simply a man of valor who, "doesn't permit a fly to walk on his nose," who will suffer nothing, and the organization to which he belongs expresses this belligerent stance:

> The Mafia is conscious of itself as a being; it is an exaggerated form of individual strength which is the unique and sole arbiter of any

conflict, clash of interests or ideas. It suffers no other superiority or arrogance.[7]

This basic element of the Mafia mentality underlies the strongly aggressive component of the phenomenon, because every action is aimed at defending honor at any cost, using the most ferocious method. It is also a mode of social mobility, which is, of course, simply a logical extension of the notion of honor to the notion of "status."

The historical context in which the Mafia developed as an organization in Sicily was that of a feudal society, which lasted in the Sicilian countryside from the Norman period of about 1000 A.D. to the middle of the last century. This social organization was characterized by the presence of a landed nobility who owned the land in huge estates for a long period.[8] The barons also owned contingents of armed guards, which supervised the work of the peasants and defended the property against attack. The situation is described by Pantaleone:[9]

> The guardians and the supervisors were always chosen from among those individuals according to their past ferocious delinquencies. The members of these private armies were given, step by step, the broad powers of their bosses, and it is easy to understand which way they were likely to exercise their powers. In this complete absence of public authority, and in this absolute power of the private baron who delegated his power to his lieutenants, it is possible to understand the basis of the birth and growth of the Mafia. The Mafia was therefore born essentially in response to the need to preserve the feudal structure in the countryside.

The private armies of conflicting estates were in constant and ferocious struggles, but they disappeared in 1812 after the abolition of feudal privileges. However, those who had been the chief representatives of the barons now became independently powerful so that a new social class emerged, something very close to a bourgeoisie, which continued to use violence to gain its end. But this time these violent methods were used against the nobility in order to force them off their land. Eventually, this "petty bourgeoisie," applying classic intimidation techniques, took, in part, the place of the nobility.

Mafia as an Organization

It is possible to identify roughly three basic manifestations of the Mafia. One is the classic stage, which prevailed up to the

1950s in Southern Italy. The second is characterized by the business perspective that changed some basic traits of the Mafia mentality by emphasizing the accumulation of money as a means to power and status (previously a value only of the nobility). The third is the American Mafia that is well known as an organization mostly used to dealing in illegal goods and services, such as alcohol, drugs, prostitution, and gambling. This type, while it developed this different orientation, nevertheless retained the traditional familial organization.

It is important to recognize at this point that, although the Mafia displays broad differentiation in activities in time and place, some basic features of the Mafia mentality remain the same. These are easily recognized as (1) the use of violence in the distribution of power, (2) the creation of strict hierarchies within the groups, and (3) the violent relationships between antagonistic groups. In the Mafia families, the patriarchal order of the traditional Sicilian family is not strictly observed; often the leader could be one of the brothers, and not necessarily the eldest, as we have seen in the movie, *The Godfather*, where the youngest son, Michael Corleone, succeeded the father even before his death. This is because the nature of Mafia leadership requires that the boss of the family is the individual who displays the psychological features more functional to the individual and collective growth of the organization. Thus, while the model of the typical family is used for day to day organization and management, its structure, in terms of succession and distribution of power, depends on its functional needs. The consequence of this interplay is a serious problem of endemic internal and external conflicts typical of all types of Mafia organizations. The institutionalization and legitimization of power, once it is obtained, and the attempt to freeze the existing distribution of power, becomes the greatest challenge to the Mafia organization's viability.

It is amazing that this thorough mix of the very traditional (that is, familial loyalty) with modern elements like competition, took place in a static society of peasants such as existed in Sicily in the last century. However, in this static world, the Mafia provided almost the only channel for vertical mobility. In other words, although the Mafia and social banditry were born at different times, they both developed a retributive and vengeful aspect. However the Mafia's predatory concern for the acquisition of totally legitimated power makes it vastly different from banditry.

Due to its strongly aggressive and competitive nature, the Mafia system is always in danger of dissolution. As a matter of fact we can compare this system to the Hobbesian state of nature—*homo homini lupus*—in which there is no principle of recognized justice because it is only violence that justifies social action. In this respect, its origin and continuation bears a striking resemblance to popular models of the origin and maintenance of the modern state.[10]

Mafia as the Mimic of the State

1. *The Necessity for order.* Scholars have noted that the mafioso phenomenon shows two different and apparently contradictory phases.[11] On the one hand, we may note the prevalence of anomic pursuit of supremacy and power where the result of this competition is established by physical force. The competitors or enemies are physically eliminated or forced out of the field. In this struggle, the Mafia, in true Hobbesian fashion, knows no limits. "If there is anything that we have learned," says the young Michael Corleone, "it is that it is possible to kill anyone." And the daily news provides constant testimony to this point of view, with an endless stream of stories relating the violent settling of accounts. On the other hand, once a mafioso reaches power, his major objective is to maintain the position of power through regulation of the internal conflict in his organization.

In both these phases, the use of violence and intimidation is common, but in the institutional phase, resort to violence seems to be less necessary because the Mafia power is able to develop social functions of different kinds, such as the mediation of conflicting interests, protection, repression, and to provide a number of goods and services. Nevertheless, the Mafia tends to present itself—no differently from the state—as always being in the position to call upon physical violence, in a typically deterrent fashion.

In order to make this threat credible, the actual use of violence, particularly of homicide, should have taken place in the early stage of the mafioso's career. Later, once he has reached a position of power, he will be able to send others to commit violence; in this way, he is more likely to remain

"untouched" by the crime. A successful Mafia career, therefore, is something of a passage from "killer" to "architect."

The actual use or threat of violence is only one component
in the process of legitimation of mafioso power, while the
other component is achieved through the positive identification of the social group with the mafiosi and their activities
conferring prestige and respect to the Mafia. Mostly in the
classic period, the relationship between mafiosi and the
broader population shows this process of identification. Indeed, the mafiosi could represent an ideal human type because they control an effective power even though they come
from a disadvantaged social class. Thus, they can express, as
well as can other social bandits, the prospect that illiterate
peasants can have a rapid career in a world, where, according
to tradition, there can be only bosses and servants—historically immutable social categories. The mafiosi have a great
liking for honorific titles, such as "Don," and on their way to
legitimation they are likely to entertain collaboration with the
authority of the state, in apparent contradiction with the
subcultural norms. In this way, from "honored men" they
become "men of order," a most civilized transformation. In
this position, they manage to regulate the conflict and the
indiscriminate use of violence. This capacity to control social
conflict is expressed in the most important Mafia function of
the classic period—mediation.

2. *Dispute Settlement.* In its traditional form, this activity
consisted of an intervention between thieves and their victims
in order to retrieve their stolen goods. In exchange for a
percentage of the goods, shared between the thieves and the
Mafia (as a compensation for the Mafia's service), almost all
the stolen goods are recovered, whereas if the regular police
were involved, the goods would be lost.[12] This kind of intervention takes place in a number of situations between individuals or groups, for example, between creditors and debtors in
order to obtain delay in payment of debts; or, on the contrary,
to accelerate payments. In other words, the Mafia displays a
function of maintaining equilibrium of the social order, and in
exercising this function displays the feature of repression of
common criminality, not uncommonly in partnership with
the state. A good example of this relationship seems to be that
of bandit and robber, which could be completely different

according to the possible utilization of the bandits to achieve the Mafia's aim.

In some cases, the Mafia may intervene during a kidnapping on behalf of the victim's family, forcing the bandits to reduce their ransom, and guaranteeing the hostage's release. Otherwise, according to the circumstances, the Mafia may collaborate with the state in order to physically eliminate the bandits. It may use the state, more or less indirectly, to reach political goals, or exploit antagonistic factions, such as the peasants in the case of Salvatore Giuliano, of whom we will read shortly.

More typically, in the next stage, when the Mafia shifts to the accumulation of wealth, it can keep bandits in the position of "workers" during the performance of kidnapping, robberies, and other criminal activities. In this case, the Mafia provides, as happened very recently in a number of kidnappings in Calabria (a province of southern Italy), enough protection for the bandits to hide in the countryside. It is clear that the possibility of fulfilling these different and contrasting social functions is connected mostly in the traditional Mafia to the extent of its growth as a social category, and particularly in its relation to the political power of the state. When it has gained control of political power, the Mafia tends to establish political relationships in order to protect its activities, illegal or not, and in this regard, the Mafia can act to support its own political candidates, thus controlling extended areas of public politics.

Mafia against the Bandits

There is an inherent difference between Mafia and bandits, although because of their penchant for violence, the two are often confused. Bandits tend to interfere and to be opposed to the Mafia activities, and to try to keep out of Mafia control. As we have noted, banditry is a phenomenon well known in peasant society, particularly at certain stages in its development. It is characterized by a strong and deep opposition to official power, demanding reciprocity for perceived wrongs. Bandits wish to exercise power, and sometimes they do manage to seize it. But the least of their priorities or programs (when they have them) is the attempt to reach a condition of equilibrium. Their project is always a model for freedom from oppression and a *weltanschaung* in which men can be more equal than they really are. Consequently, their political action does not upset the established social structure except in the case of bandits connected to a broader revolutionary movement, a program for subversion of the state, and an equalitarian ideology, as noted in chapter 8. While their efforts are always bound to an imaginary past, where the owners of the land are still owners, they behave more justly towards the peasants, and respect their rights.[13] In contrast, the Mafia's opposition to the established order is purely instrumental to achieving power itself, so that identification with oppressed groups is much less marked. In other words, the Mafia is likely to affirm its own order, and exercise repression as an organization, while keeping open the possibility for feuding factions to settle scores between themselves, creating situations that the Mafia may exploit for its own ends.

The way in which the Mafia establishes complex relationships with bandits and other figures who might threaten to upset the social order in some way is well illustrated by the story of Giuliano.

The Story of Salvatore Giuliano

In Sicily, up to the end of World War II, Giuliano was a popular bandit who championed a revolutionary and egalitarian ideology. It has been said that the critical episode that precipitated his career was his killing, on September 2, 1943, of a carabiniere who was trying to retrieve a sack of meal that Giuliano wanted to sell on the black market, while another smuggler was simultaneously set free because he had money to bribe the officer. Giuliano later formed a band with a number of fugitives from Monreale's jailhouse and started a systematic enterprise of extortion by intimidating the landowners in the Palermo countryside. After establishing his headquarters in Montelepre, not far from Palermo, he began to distribute the money he obtained from extortion among the peasants. In this Robin Hood fashion, he gained wide popular support.

At the time, Giuliano was a very strong opponent of the Mafia, which was fighting its own war with bandits and other ordinary criminals in its role as defender of property owners (for a price, of course). Several bloody encounters took place, culminating in the cruel killing of an old Mafia boss, found dead with his face covered in cow dung, a note hanging from his neck on which was written: "In this way Giuliano deals with the Mafiosi."[14] This period was also one in which the separatist ideology in Sicily enjoyed popular support, the platform being that the poor condition of the Sicilian people was due to the historical oppression of the island by the "northern invaders." It was believed that once Sicily became politically independent from the Italian nation, all its misfortunes would come to an end. This ideology served an important purpose in displacing hostility away from the true source of the island's troubles—the local political forces—and on to a distant and less well defined "enemy." At the same time it enhanced "peasant solidarity," and gave some focus to Giuliano's rather confused aggressive political ideas, which he had developed in his early twenties.

The separatist party, particularly its active right wing leaders (almost all of them coming from the old nobility and land owning class, and thus widely supported by the Mafia) adopted as their political strategy a strong position against the communist oriented peasant organization. And the Mafia, while it continued to eliminate peasants and bandits— Giuliano's main supporters—nevertheless managed to convince him and his gang to join with the separatist party in order to defeat the communist peasant organization. Giuliano continued this collaboration with other political parties through the Mafia network, even after the decline of the separatist party.[15] Indeed, he became familiar with several important political and civilian authorities of these parties, so that he began to see himself as "an important man" who, according to promises and assurances from these authorities, would be eventually acquitted of all his crimes, or at least assisted to relocate abroad, should it be necessary.

According to testimony given by his lieutenant and trusted follower, Gaspare Pisciotta in a trial some years later,[16] Giuliano was under the influence of the political bosses of the Monarchist and Christian Democratic parties when he organized the massacre of Portella delle Ginestre where, on May 1, 1947, during a popular local feast, he and his gang opened fire with automatic weapons, killing a number of peasants. Pisciotta was later poisoned in jail to prevent his revealing the truth about the complicity between some Mafia and political bosses and Giuliano's gang.[17]

After the slaying at Portella Delle Ginestre, Giuliano continued to support, but always through Mafia control, the political
activities of the above mentioned political parties. And with
the success of the Christian Democratic Party in Sicily in
1948, due partly to his support, he began to ask for rewards,
such as impunity for his crimes, or help in expatriating. But
his connection with the Mafia and the political establishment
were already too much of an embarrassment, and his elimination became necessary. This would not be an easy task, because Giuliano probably realized that, since his protectors had
not kept their promise, they would likely kill him. He had also
lost much of his original popular support, especially after the
slaying at Portella.

Isolated, and with not much time to live, Giuliano began to
retaliate by killing a number of political and Mafia leaders,
and for good measure some carabinieri. In the end, the Mafia
managed to convince the same Gaspare Pisciotta to kill
Guiliano on the night of July 14, 1950. Everything was set up
so that the death would be seen as a conflict with the carabinieri. In fact, the captain of the carabinieri was rewarded with a
promotion for having "killed" Giuliano. This procedure, according to Hobsbawm, is not unusual, and there is even a
Corsican proverb expressing it:[18]

> Killed after dead—like a bandit—by the police.

So, if he did not live as an honorable bandit, at least he could
die like one. But he was, in fact, not killed in an open duel, but
though treason, while he was asleep. Thus we see the callous
manipulation of "honor" by the Mafia. It is used purely
instrumentally, and at this turning point, one must question
whether the Mafia believed in the idea of the "honorable man"
at all. Certainly, it can be argued that from roughly this time
on, the Mafia mentality became more and more bent on
material gain and less on the accumulation of honor. Soon, the
ideal image of the mafioso—excessively modest and gentle-
manly—would be transformed into the colorful and noisy
man of wealth.

The Mafia Method: From Vengeance to Deterrence

1. *Protection*. In any period of its development, the Mafia has
always been concerned with establishing a genuine economic

basis to its organization. The classic method of economic accumulation is through protection, "a form of gain specifically of the Mafia, which consists of the claim of tributes for a pretended protection."[19] This is a special kind of extortion that can be applied to anyone who owns goods or operates a business in a given territory under control of the Mafia. The dynamics of this kind of intervention are typical. The victim is made aware that his property is in danger because of the presence of criminals who steal and do damage, but fortunately there are persons concerned for the welfare and order of the community who, for the sake of friendship, can protect him. In most cases, in areas where the Mafia has already demonstrated its potential for cruelty, this "friendly" message is understood, and normally it is the victim himself who, thankful for the interest that has been shown him, declares himself in the position to pay a percent in proportion to his real income. In this way he guarantees to himself a protection that he probably does not need but in the hope that it will be an effective protection against common criminality. In the colorful Sicilian dialect, this kind of payment is called, u pizzu, and the expression vagnari lu puzzu means to wet one's beak like a drinking bird. In this way, the "passivity" of the local inhabitants is exploited—and assured—by the Mafia.

If, for any reason, the protectee does not accept the service, a number of sanctions of progressive gravity are enforced—which may ultimately become homicide. In the system of protection we can easily note a real substitution of the Mafia function to the legal state function. For a service of protection, in which the Mafia tends to monopolize the use of force, as well as in the state, the use of general deterrence seems to be the prevalent meaning of this operation. Through the punishment of a single episode of rebellion, the majority of victims are scared into conforming to the established order. Protection money (taxes) is even demanded from them, with the promise that they will be protected from crime by the state's police.

2. *Organizational control.* At any stage in the development of Mafia power, the basic familial organization is control.[20] The primary familial kinship constitutes the central nucleus of the Mafia structure that tends to develop into a network of different familial groups, each of them acquiring external members on the basis of friendship, the *comparaggio* or common inter-

est.[21] The Sicilian dialect calls this type of enlarged familial group *cosca* which derives from the word *artichoke*, indicating a number of elements, which are the leaves, strictly bound to the central stem. The nature of the relationship is either biological or associative. In this way, many persons can join the group in order to solve, in Mafia fashion, their business problems, by using a large network of mutual aid, protection, and exchange of favors.

The dimensions of the *cosca* may differ according to the historical period and preferred activity of the Mafia at that time, but it differs mostly in relation to the capacity of the leader to control competition within the group. The dangers of being deposed, with its consequent change of hierarchical structure, is always present. Different *cosche* may thus be in a variable condition of alliance or conflict for the determination of their respective areas of influence. In return for control of the conflict, the *cosca* supplies military support to the leader.

3. *The appropriation of honor.* As a man of honor and respect, as an administrator of effective power, the mafioso loves to present himself very modestly, as a gentleman above the factions, who is likely to meet anybody or talk to anybody, offering his services "without interest." As Don Calogero Vizzini, powerful and ferocious Mafia boss of Villalba in Sicily during the classic period, who was connected to fraud, blackmail, extortion, and homicide said:[22]

> In every society there should be a category of person who fixes up situations when they become complicated.

Notwithstanding that the mafioso is likely to show himself as a fatherly and kindly figure, his prestige relies on the fact that, in the past, he murdered somebody, and he could certainly do the same thing again. In this way, he exercises social control through a typical psychology of terror that promises a punishment that inexorably will be applied to anyone who goes against his wishes. "Honor" is therefore transformed into a thinly veiled threat that everyone understands.

The man of honor tries to keep himself close to persons in privileged social categories, and in this way emulates distinct social types, such as the nobleman in the classic period, or the business man in the American Mafia. How strong this quest is for status in terms of progressive legitimation of the Mafia position, we can understand by the announcement that was written on the door of the Villalba's church the day of the funeral of Don Calogero:[23]

> From all his friends from his enemies themselves, he receives the fairest recognition: he was a gentlemen.

4. *Mafia retribution.* The mafioso in his role of gentleman counts on the recognition of his power, and uses violence only as a last resort. When the sanctions are aimed outside the organization, they normally follow a progression. For example, the owner of land, after the first "friendly suggestion," receives a number of progressively clearer threats, and a number of messages that symbolically represent the punishment he is likely to receive, for example, a cross of stones placed on his property.

In the next stage, we find the typical destruction of property or animals, and if it is not yet enough, the extreme form of sanction is likely to occur: kidnapping and mutilation (a typical slashing of the face), and eventually homicide. The dynamics of violence in the Mafia show different features according to the circumstances. In the case of a struggle between different *cosche*, resolution of the conflict follows a more direct approach, with less ritual. As in war, the aim is to destroy the enemy by forcing it away or by engulfing it.

In this process we see clearly a combination of retribution and deterrence. The source of the Mafia conflict is, as a rule, closely connected to economic interests or threats to the survival of the group. As we have already seen in our analysis of the feud, the dynamics of reciprocity in vengeance are originally due to motives similar to those found in the Mafia, but in the feud, vengeance appears as an end, rather than a means; it is a major motivation for the act. However, in the Mafia strategy, the retributive element is always connected to the utilitarian motive. The Mafia clearly reveals the functional and instrumental elements of vengeance, the early strands of which we saw in our discussion of the vengeance of Ulysses.

The instrumental factor is noticeable in almost every Mafia activity, especially within its own organization. The system of punishment against those who break the subcultural norms through treason or betrayal makes vengeance obligatory, and it is almost always accompanied by the disfigurement of the face with a knife, razor, or less commonly, with sulphuric acid. (This punishment is also often reserved for unfaithful women or rebel prostitutes.) Cutting out the tongue is currently used for those who have "squealed" to the enemies. The symbolic meaning of this mutilation needs no explanation; nor does disfiguring the face in a subcultural system in which noncollaboration is part of the image of man himself.[24]

5. *Mafia deterrence.* An essential feature of Mafia punishment is its visibility. When the violence that was preannounced by dark and terrifying messages takes material form, it is necessary that it will be known to the maximum number of persons, and the grim details of the execution explained. To this end, the mass media are particularly useful as a means of general deterrence. In this sense, the act of terror has the meaning not only of the punishment of individual vengeance, but the clear demonstration of a *capacity.*[25]

Just as many systems of social control justify punishment on the basis of deterrence, so the Mafia must provide, along with publicity, the certainty of the sanction. In other words, it must be as clear as possible that violating a norm will require punishment, no matter how long it takes to bring it about. In its popular image, the philosophy of Mafia vengeance is therefore strictly connected to the idea of inevitability. "Vengeance is a dish that is to be eaten cold" is a maxim that well expresses this view. The certainty of punishment, as we know, is an important element of the utilitarian conception of punishment in general, as Beccaria has pointed out.[26]

The deterrence thesis also argues that future crimes will be diminished in direct proportion to the degree of severity and certainty of the punishment. Again, the Mafia seems to be very close to this theoretical position—perhaps the most widely held justification for criminal punishment in our society. The inevitability of the Mafia sanction is also a guarantee of its capacity, and perhaps it is all too clear that this guarantee can be fulfilled much more effectively than it can by the modern state in a "free society." The Mafia need not be constrained by concerns for "due process."[27]

The Rise of Mafia Materialism

The intensification of conflict that has occurred in recent years in the Italian Mafia, is a sign of the difference between the classic Mafia, which lasted into the fifties in Sicily and Calabria, and the new Mafia. In a totally different context, such as the United States, we also see a cyclic progression through growth and diminution of Mafia conflict. One explanation for this phenomenon could be the changing field of activities of the organization that tends to maintain some basic characteristics such as the familial structure and the search for status. The activities in the classic period were mostly those of mediation and protection, and they were likely to occur in a limited territory. Also the "man of honor" type emulated a peasant background, and a quiet, conservative way of life.

In the new Mafia, the control of very important sectors of illegal activities such as drug traffic, and providing illegal goods and services are the main fields of activity. While the Mafia shows great flexibility in this regard, the accumulation of a large amount of capital nevertheless increases internal and external conflict. Also the human type of the new mafioso, with his ostentatious affluence is very different from that of the classical figure.

In the stage that we can define as the "business" stage, the Mafia is likely to choose a sphere of activity that promises the possibility of faster gain. The Mafia has no problem shifting operations from one sector to another, using illegal gain for legal investment and vice versa. The preferred fields of operation, especially in the U.S., are drugs, gambling, and prostitution. The history of the American Mafia (Cosa Nostra, the Syndicate) is also the history of a struggle for control over these "services." In this regard, we see the classic struggles among the families in New York. As far as Italy is concerned, according to Arlacchi, the state of war has been responsible for more than 700 deaths in the period between 1970 and 1982 in Calabria, one of Italy's southern provinces.[28] The recent and continuing case of Buscetta illustrates this heightened conflict that seems to be related to a decay of the traditional concept of the mafioso as a gentleman into the predatory businessman who will make any deal, if it will make money.

The Buscetta Case

Tommaso Buscetta, 56 years old, an important Mafia leader, was arrested in his luxurious apartment in San Paolo, Brazil, on October 25, 1983, and extradited to Italy in July 1984.[29] He faced several serious criminal charges, mostly related to the international market in hard drugs.

According to police records, he took up his brilliant career in Palermo, Sicily, in the late 1950s, working for the powerful boss of that time, Pietro Torretta. He then went to America, first operating in New York, then Mexico, Argentina, Paraguay, and Brazil. In the latter country, he controlled much of the cocaine smuggling from Peru to Bolivia, using his own air fleet, which consisted of some 200 planes. The drug was then transported to U.S. and European clients. In typical Mafia business fashion, Buscetta managed to transfer the profits of this illegal activity into his extensive legal businesses—a taxicab company, supermarkets, and pizzerias.

He was extradited to Italy for the first time in 1972, when he was found in possession of pure heroin, valued at that time, at about forty million dollars. In 1980 he was paroled, and immediately went back to Brazil where he lived until his final arrest in San Paolo. It was after this capture that he made a full confession about the Mafia activities, and he continues to cooperate with the Italian judiciary.[30] Buscetta provided extensive evidence concerning more than 100 unsolved Mafia homicides. Among the most important are those of the carabinieri's Lieutenant Colonel Giuseppe Russo (August 20, 1977); the chief of the Mobile Police Unit, Boris Giuliano, shot down by a solitary killer on July 31, 1979; the chief attorney general of Palermo, Gaetano Costa, after he signed .warrants against the Spatola, Gambino, and Di Maggio "families" in 1980; the judges Terranova and Chinnici, the latter killed when his car was blown up by a remote control device.

But probably the most impressive of all—demonstrating that the Mafia can kill "almost anyone"—was the assassination of the carabinieri's General Carlo Alberto Della Chiesa, shortly after his arrival in Palermo. Endowed with "super prefect"[31] powers and the charge to defeat the Mafia, Della Chiesa, his wife, and bodyguard were shot in his car by a Mafia commando equipped with a Soviet fully automatic military rifle (Kalashnikov), used in several other Mafia killings.

According to Buscetta's information, this bloody succession of killings was related to the progressive conversion of the traditional Mafia activities (such as smuggling of tobacco) into the more remunerative drug business, and the laundering of "dirty" money from extortion or other crimes. From the mid 1970s on, these activities led to a ferocious conflict between opposing factions, reaching its peak in the 1981–83 "war" for control of the international market in heroin. This, in turn, made it increasingly necessary to resort to violence so as to avoid the interference of the criminal justice officials in Mafia affairs.

During this "war," Buscetta (even though he was still living in South America) joined the faction composed of the Inzerillo, Badalamenti, and Bontade "families," all very strong opponents of the Greco-Marchese-Riccobono, and Corleone (coming from the town of Corleone) "families." This last faction, resorting to a number of strategic alliances with other clans, eventually managed to prevail. As a result of this internal conflict, many leaders lost their lives. Among them was the boss of the Inzerillo family, his bullet-proof Alfa Romeo pierced by the Kalashnikov's deadly shots.

Almost the entire Buscetta family was destroyed: two sons, Antonio and Benedetto on September 11, 1982; and his brother Vincenzo along with his son Benny, on September 29, 1982. About one month later, Buscetta's son-in-law Giuseppe Genova was killed in his pizzeria ("New York Place") in the commercial center of Palermo. His wife (Buscetta's daughter) narrowly escaped with her life.

According to Buscetta, the Sicilian Mafia is named "Cosa Nostra," the same as its American counterpart. It maintains the basic familial structure from which a pyramidal organization developed. At the bottom of the pyramid are the "families" with soldiers and officers, or "capidecina." Each family is headed by a "capofamiglia" or "rappresentante" assisted by a "vice" and by one or more "consiglieri." Above the "families" stands a "commissione" or "cupola" presided over by a "capo-commissione" or "segretario" consisting of representatives from the families. This type of agency operates in each of the nine Sicilian provinces. Although, as a rule, no killing should be executed without the consent of the "rappresentante" of the family controlling the area where the murder would take place, the most important assassinations are decided by the "commissione" without this consent. This was an important source of conflict leading to the 1981–83 Mafia war.

Tommaso Buscetta's confession made possible the issue of more than 360 arrest warrants, including one for the former mayor of Palermo, "Don" Vito Ciancimino, whose compromising relations with the Mafia had been suspected for a long time. Other powerful bosses of the new Mafia like the Greco's, Marchese's, Vernengo's, Riina's, Provenzano's, Riccobono's, Zanca's, along with many well known and respected businessmen of Palermo, were also on the list. His confession represented (and continues to represent) one of the most dangerous threats to Mafia survival in its entire history. Action was therefore inevitable.

On October 10, 1984, ten Mafia killers shot down eight minor figures of the local underground connected to illegal bookmaking and horseracing. They were lined up in front of a stable wall close to the slaughterhouse and killed with shotguns and automatic pistols. Although many shots were fired, nobody in the neighborhood reported anything to the police, nor did they say that they had noticed anything unusual. The bloody and spectacular fashion of this multiple execution served as a warning of the power and efficiency of the Mafia. It had begun to eliminate the persons who could confirm Buscetta's story, and, since it could not reach Buscetta in his well guarded maximum security cell, it killed his relatives and friends instead. The most recent victim was Buscetta's brother-in-law, Pietro Buscetta, 62 years old, with no criminal record, shot down by three gunmen in Bagheria, not far from Palermo on December 8, 1984. But even after this "transversal vengeance," Buscetta has said that he will not cease his collaboration with Italian justice.

The most amazing feature of this story, aside from Buscetta's incredible career, is that for the first time, a high ranking Mafia boss has agreed to collaborate with the government, breaking the traditional rule of silence. The only explanation for Buscetta's actions is that he wished to retaliate in the only way left open to him, given that the rest of his faction had been so thoroughly defeated, his family destroyed, and his own life in constant danger. He must know how difficult it is to avoid Mafia punishment. He is, according to Mafia, a traitor, guilty of the most serious "crime." On the other hand, he is considered, by the state and by part of the Italian press, to be "repented." Perhaps Buscetta seeks expiation through confession.

It is more likely that he conforms to the oldest vengeance model, which the Mafia has apparently forsaken, in order to have revenge because of the Mafia's failure to keep its agreements. No longer is he in a position to *deter* the Mafia factions, but he is in a position to reciprocate by telling the authorities everything. His confessions are thus a last attempt to restore the equilibrium and reciprocity of vengeance. The equilibrium between the various factions, we suggest, was upset by the increasing concern of each faction with the accumulation of wealth, and the use of "honor" as an instrument to justify this shift towards materialism. By appropriating honor in this way, the Mafia undermined the very basis of its own social order.

In the case of Giuliano, whose bloody retaliations were in the best Mafia tradition, the Mafia was able to respond effectively and control the vengeance of one bitterly betrayed man. However, it seems less able to cope with Buscetta. The reason appears to be that the basis of order in the new Mafia has been transformed from the *cultural* to the *material* and is therefore less predictable and less dependable because the latter is not constrained by tradition. In its progressive resort to violence in response to Buscetta's confessions, because it is unable to keep up the semblance of "honor" (as was done, for example when Giuliano was murdered), the Mafia's true motive is revealed. It is clear for all to see that the Mafia has no "code of honor." Its sole and totally consuming interest, while it has always been power, is the blatant accumulation of wealth by any means, raw violence included.

Thus we may observe an attenuation of the ideological support that, through the concepts of honor and manhood, underscored the retributive elements in the *weltanschaung* of the classic mafioso. In other words, as the Mafia evolved into a more complex social organization oriented towards more specific criminal activity, the reciprocal core of its culture progressively changed to deterrence.

Notes

1. L. Sciascia, *Il giorno della civetta* (Torino: Einaudi, 1972), pp. 118–119, our translation.

2. On this point, see P. Arlacchi, *La mafia imprenditrice* (Bologna: Il Mulino, 1983), p. 153. We have relied heavily on this extensive work throughout this chapter.

3. Most of the literature has concentrated on organized crime and particular form of the Mafia, based on a number of factors, such as the ethnic

and cultural background of the members, the structure and internal relationships of the organization, and the particular fields of criminal activity. This narrow focus applies especially to work in the United States. See for example Donald R. Cressey, *Theft of the Nation*, (New York: Harper and Row, 1969) and *Criminal Organization: Its Elementary Forms* (New York: Harper and Row, 1972), among many others.

4. It should be noted that there has probably never been a single organization called "The Mafia." But there have been many organizations displaying the single *weltanschaung*, or orientation to life that we describe in this section. See Anton Blok, *The Mafia in a Sicilian Village, 1860–1960: a Study of Violent Peasant Entrepeneurs* (New York: Harper and Row, 1974).

5. This emphasis on secrecy has sometimes been used as evidence that Mafia is connected to a long history of secret societies. Hobsbawm, *Primitive Rebels*, for example links Mafia to the Carbonari secret brotherhood, p. 192. See also David L. Chandler, *The Criminal Brotherhoods* (London: Constable, 1976). However, this approach has been strongly criticized: Gaia Servadio, *Mafioso: A History of the Mafia from Its Origins to the Present Day* (New York: Stein and Day, 1976).

6. It will be recalled that Ulysses was a transitional case: he was certainly resourceful, but at crucial moments he had to turn to an external source (the goddess Athena) for help.

7. G. Pitrè, *Usi, costumi e pregiudizi del popolo siciliano* (Bologna: Forni, 1969), vol. 2, p. 292, our translation.

8. See M. Pantaleone, *Mafia e politica*, (Torino: Einaudi, 1962), pp. 23–30.

9. M. Pantaleone, *Mafia e politica*, p. 24, our translation.

10. Indeed, in its early days some historians say it actually took the place of the state.

11. P. Arlacchi, *La mafia imprenditrice*, p. 41–42; H. Hess, *Mafia* (Bari: Laterza, 1973), pp. 90–106.

12. We see here a common role of the "professional thief" observed by scholars in different cultures and at different historical periods. Jonathon Wild was perhaps the most famous professional mediator of this type in London. However, his activities were useful and possible because there was no properly established police force. See C. Klockars, *The Professional Fence* (New York: The Free Press, 1980).

13. See Hobsbawm, *I Banditi*, pp. 21–23.

14. Pantaleone, *Mafia e politica*, p. 159.

15. These were the Monarchist and Christian Democratic Parties. Pantaleone, *Mafia e politica*, p. 160.

16. Pantaleone, *Mafia e politica*, p. 157.

17. Pantaleone, *Mafia e politica*, p. 182. His murder is considered one of the Mafia's masterpieces. The bandit was in an isolation cell with his father, with no contact with any other inmates. He always checked his food thoroughly. But on the morning of February 9, 1954, he prepared coffee with his *own* coffee machine, sharing some of it with his father and a prison guard. A few moments after he had swallowed it, he died, poisoned by a strong dose of strychnine. How it was possible to poison only Pisciotta's cup still remains a mystery.

18. Hobsbawm, *I Ribelli* (Torino: Einaudi, 1966), p. 34.

19. H. Hess, *Mafia*, p. 179, our translation.

20. An important study of the American Mafia according to this familial profile is the classic of F. A. I. Ianni, *A Family Business: Kinship and Social Control in Organized Crime* (N.Y.: Russel Sage, 1972).

21. Ianni provides a definition of "comparaggio": "At baptism each child is given two sponsors . . . The parents of the child and the godparents become comare (co-mother) and compare (co-father) to one another, and all adult members of both families partake of the relationship. The comare-compare relationship is also established informally between good friends of the same sex. All these relationships are blessed by San Giovanni, the patron saint of comparaggio. They are product of ritual kinship but the mutual rights and obligations are real and binding." See Ianni, *A Family Business*, p. 19.

22. Hess, *Mafia*, p. 192.

23. Hess, *Mafia*, p. 106.

24. Symbolic disfigurements are common throughout the world among feuding societies. See, for example, M. Wolfgang, and F. Ferracuti. *The Subculture of Violence* (London: Tavistock, 1967) for examples in South America and in central Europe.

25. H. Hess, *Mafia*, p. 154.

26. For a discussion of this point, see G. Newman, *The Punishment Response*, p. 154.

27. At the same time, the need to continuously apply punishment because always new contraventions of rules occur, seems probably against the hypothesis of the inverse relationship between the certainty and severity of punishment and crime. In this regard it is possible to notice the tension between the two models of reciprocity and obedience. When the forces of reciprocity tend to grow, the *pax mafiosa* is endangered, and this capacity of control is put in doubt. See Newman, *The Punishment Response*, chapters 8 and 13.

28. P. Arlacchi, *La Mafia Imprenditrice*, p. 184.

29. The story of Buscetta and his "confessions" has been widely reported by the Italian press. As a main source of information, we have referred to a number of leading articles of the Italian national daily, *La Republica*, September 30, October 2 and 19, and December 8, 1984.

30. Something similar to this happened in the U.S. in the mid-sixties when Joseph Valachi, a minor figure of the American Cosa Nostra, made important revelations about the structure of the Mafia and its crimes. See P. Maas, *The Valachi Papers* (New York: Putnam, 1968).

31. The highest rank for the region.

10

The Lone Avengers:
An Impossible Mission

And I swear by the spirits of my parents to avenge their deaths by
spending the rest of my life warring on all criminals.
> —Bruce Wayne, on deciding to become Batman,
> after his parents had been brutally murdered.[1]

THERE ARE THREE KINDS of lone avengers in American cultural
life. Each of them, we argue, is motivated by the elementary
sense of injustice, but each expresses this sense of injustice
uniquely, and each fulfills the needs of society at large in
different ways. Indeed, in regard to many lone avengers, we
could say that society creates them in order to fulfill its
cultural design. Most of these lone avengers do not exist in
real life; they are the fruit of fantasy and myth—the stuff that
our children absorb from television and mass marketed toys.
They are the super heroes—Superman, Batman and the various Star Wars characters whose lives are devoted to the violent
fight against evil. They comprise the first type. Their mission
is impossible since evil is all around us, criminals are diabo-
lic, often with super powers of their own. Nothing short of a
Superman can cope with them.

The second type is the alienated avenger who is part real
and part imaginary. He acts out of a sense of frustration with
the existing machinery of justice. He sees crimes go unpun-

ished, the innocent punished instead. From a sense of alienation and frustration, he adopts a lifestyle that allows him to
deal directly with these injustices. Dirty Harry, the classic
hero cop is an excellent example of the imaginary avenger. So
also is the hero in the movie *Death Wish*. But there are also
real life individuals who attempt to correct these injustices—
we gave several examples of these in the introduction. Of
these, Bernhard Goetz is the most interesting case, because he
is part real, part imaginary.

The third type is the avenging prodigy, and by this we mean
to imply that this is a real life hero, who has committed
himself totally to his task, just as a great violinist becomes a
virtuoso because of his total commitment to his instrument.
Simon Wiesenthal is an excellent (and perhaps the only)
example of this type. And, although some movies have tried to
embellish on his character, his life and mission cannot be
subordinated to fiction.[2]

The Myth of the Superhero

The hero myth, described by Otto Rank in 1909[3] as part of
what he called the "family romance," goes something like this:

> The hero is born of aristocratic parents and soon after birth is subject
> to the threat of exposure. He is usually set upon the water in a casket
> and is eventually rescued by benefactors of humble origin. As he
> matures, he discovers his aristocratic origins, is acknowledged as
> nobly born, and achieves greatness and fame.[4]

The classic superheroes in western culture are said to be
Moses (the law-giver), Oedipus (the king) and Hercules (the
superman). While there have been many attempts to interpret
the meaning of the superheroes in popular American culture
(such as their "macho" image, their expression of male latency,[5] the twin fantasy,[6] their often violent ways) very little
has been said concerning their role as avengers. Yet, almost all
of the classic heroes are motivated by this singular force.
Superman *always* gets even, and he deals with villains in a
direct and violent fashion.[7] The same is true of Batman who
carries out his mission with much more gusto and in a direct
and violent manner.

> Batman is locked into a holy war against evil in all its manifestations.
> His motivations are not generous at all. It is vengeance, a matter of
> getting even somehow, that is his justification.[8]

We are able to make a number of important observations about these superheroes. First, their mission is impossible. Evil is endless and appears in more and more grotesque forms. Even though they have special powers, god-like powers (We are tempted to compare these characters to those described in the early chapters of this book from the Greek myths), the forces of evil seem to have special powers as well. One evil criminal is defeated only to be replaced by another.

Second, while the heroes are extremely "macho" in appearance—thus appealing to the ideas of manliness that we have seen are so closely tied into the concept of honor and vengeance—they are, by and large, sexless. That is, their commitment to the pursuit of "justice" is so deep and all-encompassing, that there is simply no room for other, more human matters.[9] Third, we remarked on the obsessive traits so common to the social bandit in seeking vengeance. We see this obsessive trait very clearly in lone avengers. After all, it is virtually only they who are carrying on the fight. The rest of us are mere onlookers, pitifully helpless in the face of such massive evil.

Fourth, we mere mortals are not passive supporters in the way the peasants are said to support social bandits as described in chapter 8. Paradoxically, we are active supporters of the myth because we are so powerless. Two strong arguments favor this interpretation.

Many of these superheroes were created during the Depression, a period in which masses of people were powerless in the face of hopeless economic depression. The possibility of identifying with the superhero was perhaps enough to alleviate this feeling of helplessness.

Additionally, Freud[10] and Rank[11] have both argued that the wish to be heroic is deeply embedded in our psyches; that we will grasp at anything, especially the fantastic, to help convince ourselves that the heroic is the way out of the feeling of oppression that all people have, that feeling of having been put down, the elementary sense of injustice that we described in the first chapter.

This feeling can also be translated into the more positive yearning for freedom, also described in chapter 1. But florid and parrot-like pronouncements such as *Freedom and Justice For All*, the hallmark of the Batman television series, are close to a parody of American values and are a recognition that the graphic expressions that accompanied the super heroe's violent pursuit of vengeance are, in fact, pure fantasy, never to be achieved.[12] And our heroes *do* have freedom that we, by and large, do not. They are virtually all orphans, their parents having been killed in some past tragedy. They are freed from the tyranny of the family (from the Oedipal complex, psychoanalysts would say), which allows them the kind of freedom everyone unconsciously yearns for. There is also a clear similarity to the family backgrounds so often imputed to the social bandits we described in chapter 8.

Finally, we need to draw an important distinction between Batman, Superman, and the greatest of heroes—Moses. Moses brought laws down from the mountain—as god's messenger. As such, he was the creator, or at least the creative mechanism of an entire social order. He used these laws to establish order in the face of mounting chaos. The 20th century superheroes have no such creative task in mind. While their mission is to avenge injustice and help the needy, it is very clear that the established system of social order—that is, the existing criminal justice system—is not to be questioned. Thus, while they work at punishing criminals in a violent way (and the established criminal justice system accepts this as its due), there is never any conflict between the two. As Jonathon Kent, Superman's adoptive father, whispered to Clark on his deathbed:

> No man on earth has the amazing powers you have. You can use them to become a powerful force for the good! There are evil men in this world—criminals and outlaws who prey on decent folk! You must fight them—in cooperation with the law![13]

In this respect the super heroes of today are deeply conservative. While violence may well threaten any social order, the story is very different when it is used by the superheroes against grotesque criminals whose evil could never be in doubt. In fact, the established order receives a whitewash in comparison. The end result must be to greatly enhance the legitimacy of the idea of the state—whatever that "idea" or "image," as abstract as it must be, is in the minds of children. Thus, the yearning for power (that is, equality and justice for all) is turned in upon itself, so that obedience to an almost holy state is made all the more appealing. And it seems "just" because the state is also represented as "helpless" and "powerless" in the face of such monstrous evil. Otherwise, why would the superheroes be needed?

A discussion of lone avengers would not be complete without looking at a superhero of a quite different type, that of the wild west hero. While wild west heroes display attributes very similar to those of the superheroes, there are also some differences. The "lone gun" is a popular hero (who seems often to double as a lawman), portrayed as fighting for the cause of justice, and having superhuman qualities ("the fastest draw in the west").[14] The most important for our purposes are the two recently revived avengers, the Lone Ranger and his partner Tonto. They are important because, in contrast to the conservatism of the superheroes, these two existed outside the law, and in some respects one might say, above the law.

The Lone Ranger varies in an important way from our other western heroes. The Lone Ranger was raised by a tribe of friendly indians, and he made a close boyhood friend of Tonto. After some time, he was reunited with his family, and after many years of schooling and training in the army, forgot his indian past. One day he was on patrol with the army when they were ambushed by renegade indians, and a terrible massacre ensued. He was left to die, but as luck would have it, Tonto (a "good" indian) came along, recognized the amulet he was wearing, and nursed him back to health.

The two saw injustice all around them. They recognized that there was evil on the "white" side and evil on the "red" side. Only they, representing the good of each side, could fight the battle of good against evil and thereby ensure that justice was done. In these characters, we find the familiar characteristics of the mythical hero that we described in chapter 8: obsessive pursuit of their goal (the triumph of good over evil), a mysterious existence (the wearing of masks), motivation stemming from a precipitating, harsh, experience (the massacres of whites and indians).

Their rich and interesting epic is, however, different from the usual legends of wild west heroes in that they represent an attempt to establish themselves as a third party to intervene in the conflict between the two warring factions. This is in stark contrast to other social bandits who claimed, in varying degrees, to represent one particular faction (whether the downtrodden in general, or a particular family or clan), and this was claimed to be in and of itself a "just" cause. In contrast, the

Lone Ranger and Tonto represent neither side in the conflict, but they rather try to attain the status of a moral and just third party, and so justify their actions. We see here the semblance of an essential ingredient of "justice" that of impartiality, but once again defined in terms of the absence of partiality rather than impartiality itself, since the third party, nevertheless must act on the basis of partiality for itself. As we argued in the beginning of this book, it is not possible to define justice except in terms of injustice. Thus, the romantic legend of the Lone Ranger offers a powerful and enticing notion that "justice" is possible by contrasting the violence of the Lone Ranger's exploits with the "unjust" violence of the renegade indians and ignorant whites.

This is, perhaps, a cynical view of "justice," denying as it does, the very appealing devotion to "justice" provided us by the legend of the Lone Ranger. We must see, however, that if we affirm the Lone Ranger's "right" to administer justice, we affirm the right to administer it without the usual requirements of "due process" that western society sees as essential to prevent the third party from exercising its power in an arbitrary manner.[15]

The Lone Ranger, as the third party, cannot administer justice impartially, but rather does it personally. The romance and attractiveness of his exploits can be preserved while he acts alone, but if he were to grow—that is, become an "institution," procedures for the administration of justice would have to be laid down. All individuals who administered justice would have to be either as "super just" as the Lone Ranger, or the organization for the administration of justice would have to be a "super organization." In real life this very problem has been confronted recently with the transformation of Iran from a society organized along basically western lines, to a personalized justice developed by the Ayatollah Khomeini.[16] This raises many interesting questions concerning the role of complex organizations in society, but they would take us far afield of our present topic. It is sufficient for us to note that the affirmation of personal justice in the Lone Ranger, while it is very appealing as presented in the legend, affirming as it does, the triumph of good over evil, we must see that this is essentially an illusion, that such a triumph cannot occur, that all that can be achieved is to try to maintain a balance or equilibrium of power between opposing factions. To confuse the illusion with actuality, is to fall into "false consciousness" that the Marxists are so concerned about. While the Lone Ranger can make some small corrections to the balance between good and evil, they can only be short term solutions to an impossible, long-term problem.

And as long as they remain personal or lone solutions, the less chance there is of bringing about any change at all, and the greater the chance of the development of an additional source of oppression and violence. A good example of this is the part played by Charles Bronson in the Movies *Death Wish* and *Death Wish II*. This leads us to the second type of lone avenger.

The Alienated Lone Avenger

The similarities between the lone urban avenger and that of the wild west heroes are clearly identifiable, even purposely created in the movie. The last line in *Death Wish*, for example, is spoken by a New York detective who tells Bronson to "get out of town by sundown." The concurrent social conditions are also similar. In the wild west, there was a lack of organized, effective justice. Violence abounded. Many would argue that similar conditions exist in many of America's large cities. These conditions are described by sociologists in many different ways, but are usually summarized by the term "alienation." Ordinary people develop an acute feeling that justice is not being done. They search for and demand a solution. The lone urban avenger of *Death Wish* is the product of this alienation. His actions are precipitated by an horrendous event that affects himself and his family. He displays "super" qualities (his expertise with a gun). The difference, however, is that he does not represent a "downtrodden" class in any respect at all, but rather the alienated middle class of the inner city. This representation is achieved, not by any formally stated doctrine or ideology, but simply by his portrayal as relatively well off, a "super professional." This enables him, through the powerful medium of the movies, to convey a strong sense of "justice" while at the same time carrying out a program of personal vengeance.

The lack of limits to this vengeance is very clear. In the classical terms of reciprocity, it should have been enough for the *Death Wish* avenger to kill the two criminals in response to the murders of his wife and daughter. He is unable to stop at this, however, and seeks to "punish" many more. We have discussed this interesting attribute of vengeance—it seems impossible to satiate. It demands more and more, because it is essentially an act of power, an act of coercion, which, once tasted, is found to be sweet in comparison to the former helplessness so that the avenger must have more. No doubt the intensity of this "thirst" contributes to the obsessive manner in which avengers pursue their goal.

We have suggested that this type of avenger is part imaginary and part real. The *Death Wish* avenger is, of course, entirely ficitious. However, the yearning to see justice done appears daily in the press, as does the dissatisfaction with the effectiveness of the criminal justice system in convincing ordinary people that criminals receive "the punishment that they deserve."[17] *Death Wish* appealed to this mass frustration. Thus, when an actual event occurs, such as the Bernhard Goetz case that seems very similar to the scenes in that movie, there is the inevitable and unavoidable temptation on the part of the media (always closely in touch with what the public wants) to draw obvious comparisons.

In the Goetz case, the similarities were quite remarkable. The event occurred in one of New York's seamy subways; his supposed attackers were young blacks who accosted him in a way very like the movie; Goetz appeared to have been "ready for them," having purchased a gun quite some time before. He had even experienced the injustice of the criminal justice system when he was previously mugged, only to find that he, as the victim, spent far more time in the police station than did the offender. Headlines in the national and New York City newspapers immediately hailed Goetz as the "Deathwish Vigilante." One of us was in Australia at the time of this news event—and it was reported on the national news even there. The universal acclaim for his act of vengeance was indeed remarkable. However, unlike the movie, real life events began to take place that interfered with the imaginary construction of this heroic act of vengeance perpetrated by Goetz, the unofficial representative of the alienated urban dwellers of New York.

First, leaders of minority groups began to cry "racist." At about the same time, Goetz turned himself in and gave a long interview explaining his actions. Unlike the daunting figure of

Charles Bronson, Goetz turned out to be a rather pale, bespec-
tacled person, mild and unaggressive. Although some tried to
paint him as "paranoid" and "crazy," the fact is that the more
that was revealed about his past and his friends, the more
ordinary he became. He was not a superhero after all. Now a
conflict between reality and fantasy emerged. The grand jury
refused to indict Goetz for attempted murder as requested by
New York District Attorney, Robert Morgenthau. It handed
down only an indictment for illegally carrying a handgun (a
crime unknown in other parts of the United States).

Perhaps because Goetz did not fit the preconceived image of
the superhero, the media began to listen to the cries of minority leaders, who at last managed to focus some attention on the
physical injury done to the four youths, one of whom was
irreparably brain damaged. While the media had focused on
the fact that the four youths had previous police records, and
that they were carrying "sharpened screwdrivers," celebrated
author and journalist Jimmy Breslin had the temerity to correct Phil Donahue by pointing out that only two of the youths
had screwdrivers, and that they weren't sharpened. The press
also "discovered" that Goetz had fired a fifth shot into the last
youth, to whom he had said something like, "You don't look
so bad, here's another!" This information had been available
for at least a month before, but none of the media reported it.[18]

Suddenly, the issue became a *legal* issue of whether or not
Goetz had shot in self-defense. Yet this was surely not the
basis of the hero worship heaped on Goetz by the media up to
this point. In actual fact, the vengeance motive had until now
been the focus of the media, and what had made his acts
"newsworthy."[19] The fact that he fired the fifth shot was
entirely consistent with the *Death Wish* mentality of vengeance.

As we write, a second grand jury has been empanelled and
has indicted Goetz for attempted murder. What should we
expect? Unlike the other cases described in the introduction of
this book, where, even when found guilty, vengeance offenders received light sentences, we expect Goetz to suffer severe
punishment. There are two reasons for this. First, he has not
lived up to the superhero image expected of him. He has
neither a fantastic physical prowess or macho looks. Nor is he
an aggressive type of personality, as far as one can see. While
there has been some media attempt to portray him as an

"electronics whiz," in actual fact, his life seems to be quite ordinary by New York standards. Second, because of the strong voice being heard on behalf of the "offender/victims," it is likely that the direct and arbitrary nature of Goetz's justice (this aspect indeed typical of the super hero), will not be tolerated. Indeed, the more this is played up, the more the court will view his actions seriously. His acts cannot be compared to the vengeance killings described in the introduction, which were intensely *personal* (that is, the father kills the kidnapper of his son). Rather, he is portrayed as the lone, alienated avenger who has done something only a crazy person would do, given that his mission is absolutely impossible—for how can he avenge all the injustices of criminals against victims that occur in New York every day? Such a mission would make sense only if everyone else joined in to help. This is what frightens the established justice system; he has acted out, not on his own behalf but on behalf of all other alienated citizens of New York. Therefore, his vengeance is public, not private. Because he is not a superhero, because this is not a fantasy, this vengeance cannot be tolerated by the state. It is direct competition, displaying as it does the ineptitude and inadequacies of the established justice system. His punishment will therefore be severe.[20]

There is one final difference between Goetz and a superhero. He does not display *commitment*. While the problem of surviving in New York City may have been on his mind more than those who live in the less harried suburbs, it is apparent that he has not (as yet) devoted his life to avenging the gross injustice committed by the criminals of New York. The hero in *Death Wish* did indeed become more and more obsessed with his mission. And we have argued that this is an important feature of both imaginary superheroes, and those that are part real, part fantasy (such as the social bandits like Jesse James). In this respect, Goetz again fills the bill of the "failed hero." In contrast, our next type comes very close to filling the role of a real life hero.

Simon Wiesenthal:
The Avenging Prodigy

The enormity of the challenge that confronted and still confronts Simon Wiesenthal, the famed Nazi hunter, is best summed up by Adolf Eichmann: "One hundred dead is a catastrophe. Five million dead is a statistic."[21] Wiesenthal came to see that it would take more than violence, simple revenge or blind rage of the kind that drove Achilles to avenge his friend's death to solve the problem stated so succinctly by Eichmann. Wiesenthal has, over his forty years of Nazi hunting, made many enemies who have tried to impune his motives. When asked about his life devotion to revenge, his most common reply is:

> I'm doing this because I have to do it. I am not motivated by revenge. Perhaps I was for a short time in the very beginning. At the end of the war, when I was liberated after almost 4 years in a dozen concentration camps, I had little physical strength left, but I did have a strong desire for revenge. I'd lost my whole family. My mother had been taken away before my very eyes. I thought my wife was dead.[22]

The remarkable thing is that, while many other Jewish groups straight after the war began programs of direct and violent vengeance against the Germans, and Wiesenthal, over the years, has been invited many times to join with such groups, he has steadfastly refused. These groups were undoubtedly out for revenge, as the following statement from a member of the Jewish Brigade attests: "We'll have just one program— we'll burn down . . . houses . . . kill . . . rape women."[23] It is Wiesenthal's refusal to adopt this violent stance in his lifelong pursuit of evil that separates him from the superheroes. While in fantasy, direct violence seems to have a most satisfying effect upon the consumers of the myths, Wiesenthal saw that in reality violent acts could never succeed in any way in countering the terrible atrocities of the Nazis. That is, to properly balance the evil, it would have been necessary for him to perpetrate six million killings to make up for the six million murders committed by the Nazis. This was the clear impossibility of his task, putting aside the question, sometimes unfairly raised against him, that to commit such violence might somehow make him similar to the Nazis. As Wiesenthal noted, "Murder can never be excused by another murder. One cannot 'balance' crimes . . . murder does not expiate murder."[24]

The Story of Wiesenthal

Wiesenthal was born in 1908 in Lvov, Austria, and was educated as an architectural engineer at the University of

Prague.[25] At the beginning of World War II, his stepfather was arrested by the Soviet secret police and eventually died in prison, and his stepbrother was shot. Simon Wiesenthal managed to save himself, his wife, and his mother from deportation to Siberia, by bribing a commissar. When the Germans displaced the Russians in 1941, Simon Wiesenthal and his wife were sent to a concentration camp outside Lvov and both were eventually assigned to a forced labor camp. Unbeknown to the Wiesenthals, throughout Europe the Final Solution had begun.

By September of 1942, a total of eighty-nine members of the families of Simon Wiesenthal and his wife had perished. Because his wife's blonde hair gave her a chance of "passing," Simon Wiesenthal was able to make a deal with the Polish underground and spirited her out of the camp in the autumn of 1942. She lived in Warsaw undetected for two years.

Simon Wiesenthal himself escaped in October 1943 but was recaptured in June 1944 and sent to a camp where he most certainly would have been killed had the eastern front not been collapsing under the advance of the Russian army. Knowing that they would be sent into combat if they had no prisoners to justify their rear-echelon assignment, the SS guards decided to keep the few remaining inmates alive.

Very few of the prisoners survived the German westward retreat and winter marches from concentration camp to concentration camp, which ended at Mauthausen in Upper Austria. Weighing less than 100 pounds, Simon Wiesenthal was one of the 34 prisoners still alive, out of the original 149,000 when Mauthausen was liberated by the American armored unit on May 5, 1945.

Once his health was restored, Simon Wiesenthal began the task that would become his life's work. He gathered and prepared evidence on Nazi atrocities for the war crimes section of the United States Army and also worked for the Army's office of strategic services and counter-intelligence corps. He headed the Jewish Central Committee of the United States Zone of Austria. Late in 1945, Simon Wiesenthal and his wife Cylia—both of whom thought the other to be dead—were reunited. Simon Wiesenthal ended his association with the United States army in 1947, and opened the Jewish Historical Documentation Center in Linz to assemble evidence for future trials.

As the cold war developed, both the United States and the Soviet Union lost interest in prosecuting Nazi war criminals. His frustrated volunteers and supporters drifted away, he closed the Linz office in 1954, and gave the information he had accumulated to the government of Israel. One dossier he kept for himself; the one on Adolph Eichmann, the inconspicuous technocrat who, as chief of Gestapo's Jewish section, supervised the implementation of the Final Solution.

He never relaxed his pursuit of the elusive Eichmann and finally, in collaboration with Israeli agents, Eichmann was captured in Argentina and brought to trial in Israel. Found guilty of mass murder, Adolph Eichmann was executed on May 31, 1961.

Encouraged by his success in the Eichmann case, Simon Wiesenthal reopened the Jewish Documentation Center in Vienna and concentrated exclusively on the capture of Nazi war criminals, including the hated Dr. Joseph Mengele, the infamous "Angel of Death" of Auschwitz, the personification of Nazi sadism and ruthlessness.[26] On the basis of information collected by Wiesenthal's Center for Documentation, Mengele's Paraguayan citizenship, granted in 1959, was revoked in 1979 after the intervention of the United States Congress. However, Mengele was supported by a network of surviving former Nazis known as Die Spinne (The Spider).[27] The challenge to catch Mengele drove Wiesenthal.

> Mengele is responsible for the death of 400,000 people, 150,000 of them children. How can one pay for 400,000 deaths? We have set aside $100,000 to encourage his bodyguards to sell him. He can't sleep anywhere for long and must always look over his shoulders. His friends are dying off. So, his very life is now a sentence.[28]

Fate worked against Wiesenthal. Mengele died before Wiesenthal—now in his mid-seventies—could bring him to justice.

Wiesenthal, the Lone Avenger

The international press commonly refers to Wiesenthal as the "avenging angel." The motives of raw vengeance are often imputed to him. "He is driven by a fierce desire to avenge those whose blood still cries out for justice and retribution."[29] But as we noted earlier, Wiesenthal, while admitting to raw vengeance as the precipitating motive to his life's work, is careful to show that this motive was only viable for only a few years. After that time, his task was *greater* than that of raw vengeance. Yet he does not wish to advance what one might see as the opposite to vengeance—forgiveness.

> Revenge is not my motivation . . . but through forgiveness you may open the door to the next holocaust . . . I have 6 million clients . . . You can forgive crimes against you personally, but no one is authorized to forgive crimes against others . . . I have a warning that the murderers of tomorrow will never have any rest.[30]

What, then, is Wiesenthal's mission? The answer lies in an understanding of the role of vengeance in history, because Wiesenthal's quest is nothing less than to change the course of history, or at least, prevent it from repeating itself. "Human history repeats," he says. "When you know history you will recognize the danger."[31]

We have seen throughout this book that vengeance is a process. One act of violence is returned for another, and the cycle continues until one side is annihilated. While in its less sophisticated forms this cycle is immediate in the sense that the wronged parties aim to reciprocate as quickly as possible, we have seen that the more mature form takes history very seriously. A wronged party may wait for years to get even, and the cycle of vengeance may last over many generations. In other words, vengeance does not allow one to forget, and it is only through forgetting that forgiveness can truly be made possible. The vengeful act itself ensures that it will be repeated.

And here we discover a fascinating possibility. We must realize that history repeats itself, not because it has a poor memory, but because of the very opposite. And if the past acts of vengeance have been violent, the future acts, we know, will be more so. Thus, Wiesenthal is faced with a truly difficult historical problem: how to carry out vengeance and at the same time ensure that the same thing will not happen again? Wiesenthal's solution was to depersonalize vengeance and make it a matter of public responsibility. We see that this is an important step in elevating himself beyond the level of a mere individual to become a super individual. But it also "sterilizes" vengeance so that it becomes something else—a warning, Wiesenthal calls it, and in that sense, an attempt at deterrence. As Wiesenthal points out:

> Think of Eichmann. He could have been executed without a trace in Argentina. But the Israelis knew it was necessary to drag him across the ocean and risk antagonizing world opinion and be accused of violating international law. Why? because Eichmann HAD TO BE TRIED. The trial was more important than the defendant. Eichmann was already a dead man when he entered the courtroom. But the trial would convince millions of people, those who knew nothing or who did not want to know.[32]

But now we see the impossibility of his task, and perhaps also, why he is so much alone in his mission. The impossibility stems from the fact that he must convince governments to take on the role that he personifies. But governments change, and they do not have *feelings* in the sense that Wiesenthal has. Governments are more concerned with using punishment to maintain order. They will use vengeance (retribution) only in so far as it fulfills that aim. Thus, in order to turn vengeance into deterrence, Wiesenthal must either depend on the unreliable support of governments to carry out punishment, or he must develop an organization capable of doing the same thing. Such an organization would have to take on characteristics of the state. But Wiesenthal rejected the direct use of violence, and the organization that he has developed is hardly an organization at all. Rather, it seems to be a loosely knit network of informants and volunteers. There is no formal structure to his organization. He is therefore, very much a lone avenger, having carried on his task essentially as an individual.[33]

Yet it would seem that the enormity of the task is such that only governments in their size and resources could even begin to deal with it. Again, as Wiesenthal notes,

> I saw Adolph Eichmann for the first time on the opening day of his trial in the courtroom in Jerusalem. For nearly sixteen years I had thought of him practically every day and every night. Fifteen times, after each item of indictment, Eichmann was asked whether he was guilty. Each time he said, "not guilty" . . . I thought that Eichmann should have been asked six million times (one time for each person whose death he had caused) and he should have been made to answer six million times . . . The Eichmann trial proved the inadequacy of human law. The criminal codes of all civilized nations know the definition of murder. The lawmakers were thinking of the murder of one person, or two, or fifty, or maybe a thousand persons. But the systematic extermination of six million people blasts the framework of all law.[34]

Not only is vengeance against such acts not *humanly* possible, it is not even possible for governments to carry out. One might even say that it is less possible for governments, since they are so sensitive to the use of power, wishing to preserve it only for the maintenance of their own order, and not as vengeance on behalf of others. Thus, while many Nazi criminals have been caught as a result of Wiesenthal's efforts, the work is far from complete, and in some cases even when Nazi criminals have been caught, their punishment has been less than what their crimes may have warranted. Italy has recently released a Nazi war criminal on grounds of "ill-health." Was such "compassion" shown for victims of the holocaust? Furthermore, Wiesenthal estimates that some 15,000 to 20,000 Nazi criminals are still free and living in South America, Spain, the Near East, Germany, and other countries. There is little chance now that many of these will be caught. But Wiesenthal pushes on, driven by a deep and personal sense of injustice, pushing himself in his old age, beyond human limits:

> When we come to the other world and meet the millions of Jews who died in the camps, and they ask us, what have you done? There will be many answers. You will say, I became a jeweller. Others will say, I smuggled coffee or American cigarettes. Another will say, I built houses. But I will say, I did not forget you.[35]

Notes

1. Arthur Asa Berger, *The Comic Stripped American* (New York: Walker and Co., 1973).

2. For example, Ira Levin's *The Boys from Brazil*, although there is the tendency to sensationalize Mengele in this and other movies.

3. Otto Rank, *The Myth of the Birth of the Hero: A Psychological Interpretation of Mythology* (New York: Robert Brunner, 1952), first published, 1909.

4. Andrew Lotterman, "Superman as a Male Latency Stage Myth," *Bulletin of the Meninger Clinic*, 45 (1981):6, pp. 491–98.

5. Lotterman, Superman, pp. 491–98.

6. D. Burlingham, "The Fantasy of Having a Twin," *Psychoanalytic Study of the Child*, 1 (1945):205–10. Superman's twin is Clark Kent. The Wondertwins have taken this fantasy even more to the extreme; they are able to change form at will.

7. For a discussion of Superman's vengeance in the movie *Superman II*, see G. Newman, *Just and Painful* (New York: Macmillan, 1983). See also E. N. Bridwell, *Superman from the Thirties to the Seventies* (New York: Crown, 1971).

8. Berger, "Batman and the Archaic Ego," in *The Comic Stripped American*, p. 161.

9. It is true that the purity of Superman's character has been tampered with in recent years. He appears, more and more, to have human psychological characteristics such as anger, love for Lois Lane, and the need to rest after a day's work. In this regard, the folly of the twentieth century is revealed—the problems of life cannot be solved by physical force alone.

10. S. Freud, "Moses and Monotheism: Three Essays," standard edition of the Complete Works of Sigmund Freud, trans. James Strachey (London: Hogarth, 1964).

11. Ibid.

12. This is, of course, why they are comic book characters, and not characters of classic novels. Comics *are* a parody after all.

13. Bridwell, Superman, p. 207.

14. See Orrin Klapp, *Heroes, Villains and Fools*, (Englewood Cliffs, N.J.: Prentice-Hall. 1962).

15. We have outlined this problem in our analysis of the Mafia.

16. See G. R. Newman, "Khomeini and Criminal Justice," *Journal of Criminal Law and Criminology* 73, 2 (1982):pp. 561–81.

17. See Newman, *Just and Painful* for many examples.

18. *20/20*, March 21, 1985.

19. After all, many violent incidents, more severe than this one, occur in New York City everyday.

20. We make this prediction, presuming that he will be found guilty. And this, of course could turn out not to be the case, since he should be able to make a spirited case for "self defense." The outcome of guilt is determined by other factors, unrelated to the question of punishment. So there is also a reasonable chance he will be found innocent.

21. Wiesenthal, *Murderers Among Us*, p. 98.

22. Wiesenthal, *The Murderers Among Us*, p. 8.

23. M. Bar-Zohar, *The Avengers* (New York: Hawthorn, 1967), pp. 21–22.

24. Wiesenthal, *Murderers Among Us*, p. 9.

25. This brief biographical sketch is taken from Simon Wiesenthal Center for Holocaust Studies, on the campus of Yeshiva University of Los Angeles.

26. Among the many sadistic "experiments" conducted by Mengele were his twin studies in which he used painful injections to attempt to change the color of their brown eyes to blue; injection of eyes, spine and brains with camphor; draining the blood of children for study; cutting off body parts of female prisoners for tissue cultures. See *The Murderers Among Us*, pp. 154–57; *New York Times*, January 23, 1985.

27. Mengele has assisted Paraguayan police in hunting down the Ache' indians to reduce them to slave labor, using methods chillingly reminiscent of the German work camps: *Time Magazine*, September 26, 1977. In addition to being a mutual protection society, Die Spinne specializes in extortion and smuggling in South America.

28. *USA Today*, April 21, 1983. The reward for Mengele's capture had been 3.4 million dollars, *Newsweek*, May 20, 1985.

29. *Canadian Jewish News*, Toronto, No. 36, p. 142, 1982.

30. *People*, November 1977.

31. *The Racquette* "I'm not a James Bond or Don Quixote," State University College of Potsdam, New York: Vol. 51:9, November 20, 1980.

32. Wiesenthal, *The Murderers Among Us*, p. 73.

33. There are other Nazi hunters, some much younger than he. Charles Allen, probably the best known of these, currently works on uncovering the American Nazi war criminals. *Jewish World*, March 14, 1985.

34. Wiesenthal, *The Murderers Among Us*, pp. 96–98.

35. *The Washington Post*, April 1, 1979.

Conclusion

THROUGHOUT THIS BOOK, we have analyzed some manifestations of vengeance in western culture in its individual and collective forms, to suggest a possible development from ancient times to the present. Our journey, unlike that of Dante, does not seem to take us from vengeance to forgiveness and salvation, but rather to different expressions of the same basic vengeful feelings. By returning to their original source, we may shed some light on the nature of this apparently contradictory phenomenon.

We posited that all forms of vengeance arise from an elementary sense of injustice, deriving from the original relationship of dominance-submission. This very archaic relationship provokes two intertwined and antithetical responses: the one of rebellion in its reciprocal form, and the other of conformity, in terms of obedience necessary for the maintenance of the social order.

However, while the wide development and enforcement of the obedience response is quite understandable in terms of supporting this essential social need, the logic of reciprocity seems less clear and in need of further explanation.

It is clear from all the stories we have analyzed previously that reciprocity is the essential element of vengeance. That is to say, as far as the vengeful exchange is concerned, a "wrong" must be repaid with another "wrong."

But how can one wrong be corrected by another? By insisting on an "equal" punishment (a life to make up for a life), vengeance (or justice) merely takes away another life. Because of this, opponents of the death penalty say that the punishment of death, instead of "correcting" the crime, merely "adds" one wrong to another.

We can take this argument one step further, taking into

164

account Christ's admonition to "turn the other cheek." Should we not forgive the criminal, or at least return a lesser amount of punishment to him in comparison to the damage done by his offense? But if we do this, the "just deserts" of vengeance are no longer "just," for the essential element of justice in this model of equality (that is equal punishment for equal crime) has been violated.

Where, then, is the logic of the supposed moral exchange that occurs between the offender and the punisher? How is the evil of his act put aright—either by making the offender suffer the same amount of pain as that which he inflicted on his victim, or by "letting him off?" The dynamic of vengeful action is aimed at undoing the offender's act. But since it is clear that acts, once committed, cannot be undone, not even by rewards,[1] we are forced to conclude that the "logic" in this exchange has a very special structure, one that closely resembles magic.

The Magic of Vengeful Exchange

Erich Fromm[2] has speculated that the notion of vengeance is a product of magical thinking. We know that magic plays a central role in the thinking of children and neurotics. By such thinking it is possible to transcend the ordinary constraints of logic; to animate things; turn ideas, acts, into their opposites. Magical transformations of the external world are made possible, indeed made necessary, by a process that Fromm argues is similar to that of the psychological mechanism of envy. In fact this mechanism seems to have importance for the perception of immediate injustice.

The biblical version of humanity's first homicide provides some support for this thesis. As we know, it was Cain who, with his brother Abel, presented the fruits of their labor to their Master, and it was Abel who was favored. The motives for the Master's preference can only be guessed, but it is possible that he wanted to put Cain to the test (as later happened to Abraham) to see at which point Cain would cease to obey his authority. This test was surely unjust. But Cain chose the most radical course of action: to eliminate the brother and with him the frustration of confronting a grave threat to his self-esteem. The terms of envy and jealously indicate the same state of frustration—aggression. The ego is reduced in self-image, having to compare itself unfavorably with other privileged persons according to a system of values that are nevertheless shared by that same ego. Envy, a very common sentiment, also produces many reactions that are not necessarily destructive. In a society that is based on a highly competitive value system, it also means that one may improve one's self-image, perhaps inevitably, at the expense of others. Perhaps this is the most general, yet most true, product of the feeling of envy. In the face of failure or when one is "wronged," the social and psychological mechanisms are unable to compensate for the resulting imbalance. Envy invokes aggression that may be directed against the self, or is more easily displaced against the object that has "disturbed" the balance, thus attempting to neutralize it.

There is a difference between the psychodynamic mechanisms of envy and vengeance. We may observe in vengeance the existence of a real "offense," an act that determines or which is then at once determined by the damage it causes; in envy, aggression is more psychological and less easily recognized as aggression by the subject who is suffering. The individual will typically devalue the characteristics of the object of envy, in an effort to reestablish the balance. Should the balance not be reached (we have seen that this is unlikely), jealousy of intense proportions may arise, eventually producing a deep anxiety or fear of destroying the same loved person. This view derives from an impossible contradiction: that the loved one must prefer a person valued as "better," this preference not infrequently determined by the vengeance mechanism (e.g. murder by a slighted lover is celebrated in literature and in the criminal courts of most societies).

In both cases, this seems to be an intense reaction to aggression in an effort to diminish the impact on one's own self-esteem. Such aggression is in turn felt as profoundly unjust and, in the strategy used to neutralize it, appears at the same time to give rise to the psychological elements that produce vengeful passion.

Vengeance and the Desire for Omnipotence

The desire for omnipotence, deriving from the tendency to unlimited expansion of the ego, is a possible explanation of the "irrational" drive to retaliate. This tendency seems to go beyond the simple proportioning mechanisms of "a wrong for a wrong." Rather, as we have argued, the vengeful act also contains within itself a rebellion against authority, and it is from here that the excessive intensity of the force for vengeance derives. This process figures strongly in the images we construct of the lone avenger who is able to polarize currents of collective identification. It is through this deep yearning for omnipotence, which every child experiences and all adults dream of, that superheroes gain their profoundly significant relationship with vengeance.

Many forms of aggression may be thought of as attempts to secure the ego from attacks on its integrity, or threats to one's self-esteem (autonomy). Such attacks are seen primarily as issuing from a powerful person whose decisions are arbitrary and incomprehensible. It is against this person, that destructive power is directed first in a vain attempt to liberate the ego, and subsequently to substitute oneself for the oppressor. These feelings run very deep. The injustice to which we all seem victims every time we are "corrected" or do something wrong is, in reality, the sense that it is inevitable and deeply connected to the maintenance of social order. Vengeance is an attempt to deny this condition of helplessness against the imposition of social rules. But moral restraints against such action are internalized so that the reaction of aggression becomes displaced against other "enemies" who are substituted for the original object.

Rebellion in its most primitive form is therefore much different from its more advanced socially organized form in which it takes on an ideological tenor that justifies a common action against the established order and seeks to substitute one that is more just.

In its primitive form, vengeful rebellion satisfies only the desire for private elimination of the aggressor, and may take on crude aspects. We have seen, however, that this form of rebellion nevertheless lies at the bottom of all rebellions. We see a good example of this process in the transformation of the prepolitical form of rebellion, social banditry, into a broader revolutionary movement where a reciprocal ideology prevails. On the other hand the enforcement of obedience seems to show a kind of "parallel" refinement toward more and more sophisticated ideological forms in the development of the idea of expiation. It is again worth noticing the deeply contradictory nature of these processes whose conflict, we have argued, could be regarded as a main source of the dynamic of the social order.

Epilogue: The Ghost of Vengeance

In the so called developed societies we see the obedience model played out to a great extent in the form of collective consent. Although the degree of such consent may vary considerably according to the particular social setting, and consequently the use of coercion to maintain the social order may be more or less noticeable, developed societies can be regarded as "obedient" societies. In its present social form the source of oppression becomes progressively less recognizable, partly because of increasing psychological repression and partly because of the more and more abstract character of authority. Under these conditions, the need for reciprocity is forced into a more abstract form producing what we can call the "ghost of vengeance."

In order to ensure that there is "Freedom and Justice for All" the superheroes, as we have read, are forced into the endless and impossible task of "getting even" with Evil. As a result they seem to change vengeance into obedience, creating a totally appeased world under the surveillance of the forces of Good, and a parodoxical destiny for an originally subversive feeling. Moreover, the real (or almost real) characters of this superheroic model face an impossible task. However resolute and violent the reactions of the superheroes are, they nevertheless result from a feeling of social powerlessness, but they are able to keep alive the idea that ordinary people can put wrongs right.

The accomplishments of the lone avengers are modest. The solitary gunman in his nightly ride through the dark labyrinth of New York's subway is unable to restore the balance between good and evil. On the contrary, he is likely to be prey to social control agencies such as the media and the criminal justice system, which could easily change his exploits into the misdeeds of an ordinary street criminal.

Perhaps there is no way for individual efforts to change the course of history. We noted this difficulty concerning Wiesenthal's mission—at least from the retributive point of view. Nor was it possible for the great Achilles in his shining armor to alter the course of events in the Battle of Troy. It was as though his role in history was—how shall we say it—preordained?

Notes

1. It is the unhappy condition of humans, some modern psychoanalytical theorists would say, to be chained to the past. This is why whole religions have arisen in an effort to cancel out past sins (that is, to cancel out guilt). Almost all of these religions advocate pain and suffering as the effective weapons against guilt. It will be remembered that each of Dante's seven Ss was erased from his forehead as he proceeded through the successive stages of Purgatory.

2. E. Fromm, *The Anatomy of Human Destructiveness* (New York: Holt, Rinehart and Winston, 1973), p. 273.

Index

A

Abbott, J. H., 122
Achilles, 24–33, 53, 104, 117
    wrath of, 24–27
Adorno, T. W., 46, 47
Aegisthus, 42–44
Aereopagus, 43
Aeschylus, 42, 44–45, 47
Agamemnon, 24–30, 32, 34, 42–44,
    47, 53
Aggression, types of, 7
Albany Times Union, 8
Alcinous, 37
Anderson, J., 101
Angiolillo, P. F. M., 122
Antinous, 40, 41
Apollo, 25, 31, 32, 43, 44
Archbishop Roger, 48–51
Arensberg, C., 100, 102
Areopagus, 41
Arlacchi, P., 143–145
Arnold, O., 122
Athena, 26–28, 39–41, 43
Atreus, 42

B

Bancroft, G., 121
Bandit. *See also* Social bandit
Bar-Zohar, M., 162
Beccaria, C., 138
Becker, E., 13, 22
Beltran, E., 123
Berger, A. A., 161–162
Billingsley, P., 123
Billy the Kid, 103. *See also* Social
    bandit
Black, D., 8, 122

Black-Michaud, J., 90, 92, 98–102
Bloch, M., 86
Blok, A., 144
Bradley, L. C., 123
Bridwell, E. N., 161
Brill, A. A., 23
Briseis, 26, 30
Brown v. U.S., 121
Burlingham, D., 161
Burns, W. N., 123
Buscetta, T., 139–43
Busquet, J., 101, 102

C

Calchas, 25, 29
Calliope, 24
Calypso, 37
Campbell, J. K., 101–102
Canadian Jewish News, 163
Carfagno, V., 86
Centralia massacre, 110
Chandler, D. L., 144
Choephori, 42
Christie, N., 8
Chryse, 25, 26
Chryseis, 25
Chrysippus, 42
Circe, 38
Claudius, 60–63, 65
Clytemnestra, 42, 44, 45, 53
Civil War. *See also* Social bandit
Code of Islam. *See also* Vengeance
    individualization of responsibil-
        ity, 75
    god as avenger, 74–75
Codino, F., 34–35
"Conscience collective," 10

Contrition as symbolic payment, 52
Coser, L., 91, 101
Cressy, D. R., 144
Crime
  ambiguity of definition, 3–7
  ambiguity of punishment, 4
  criminal as hero, 107–21
  dynamics of primal crime, 16
  guilt, 19
  justifiable as group act, 16
  rebellion vs. authority, 18
  social control, 6
  symbolic substitution, 16
  "totemic" feast, 16
  treason, the worst offense, 55–56
Criminal as hero. See also Social
    bandit
Cultural conflict, 21
Cultural guilt, 17
Cultural traits of the bandit, 114–19
  basic motivation, 114
  conflict, 117–18
  destroyed by treason, 116–17
  god-like qualities, 115–16
  honor, 118–19
  obsessive, 118
Cumming, J., 46
Cyclopes, 11, 12, 35, 38–40

D

Dante, A., 46–58, 169
  Dante's Hell as vengeance, 46–58
  Hell, 50–51
  Inferno, 48–58
  Purgatory, 51–52
  three zones of hell, 55
Death Wish, 152–155. See also Lone
    avenger; Vigilante
Dejeux, J., 122
"Delphic Code," 43, 52
Dimsdale, T. J., 122
Durham, M. E., 101
Durkheim, E., 8, 19–20, 23

E

Electra, 42, 44
Engelen, T. L., 122
Eumenides, 45
Exodus, 1

Expiation
  aspects of, 45–46
  discovery of, 45–46
  as vengeance, 51–53

F

Feud
  cattle stealing, 78
  compensation, 70, 71
  condition of total scarcity, 90–91
  conflict, authority v. collective
    action, 92–93
  conservative people, 104
  continuity as vengeance, 99–100
  criminal as hero, 107–21
  cultural mythology, 106. See also
    Myths
  definition, 69
  delicate balance, 69–70
  differences based on cultures, 106
  economic factors, 80, 90–91
  equity and heirarchy, 92–93
  fear of aggression, 92
  fear of starvation, 91–92
  funerary dirges, 99
  historical origins, 71–74
  honor and power as synonymous,
    97
  honor and shame, 95–98, 104
  Middle East. See The Middle East
  "organized violence," 69. See also
    Vengeance
  Ozarks, 72
  paradoxical view, 107–121
  political factors, 80
  property, 105
  "pure feud," 69
  Sardinia, 76–87
  social control, 98–99
  substitute of legal redress, 104
  in Texas, 103–107. See Texas
  violence as driving force, 94–95
Ferracuti, F., 81, 87–88, 145
Freud, S., 9, 16–17, 22, 23, 55, 59,
    68, 86, 148, 162
Fromm, E., 1–3, 6–7, 19, 165, 169

G

Garza, H. A., 123
Garn, S., 59

Garrett, P. F., 121
Gerber, R. J., 47
Gerth, H., 35
Girard, R., 86
Giuliano, S. *See also* Social bandit
   story of, 132–134
Goebel, Jr., J., 86
Goetz, B. *See also* Vigilante, 2, 4, 6,
   7, 147, 153
   superhero, 154–155
Goffman, E., 46
Gravel, P. B., 122
Guelfs, 48
Guzman, M. L., 123

H

Hamlet, 13, 57, 60–70, 117
   civilized vengeance, 69
   guilt neutralization, 64–65
   Hamlet's procrastination, 60–68,
     107
   identity crisis, 96
   psychic conflict, 61
   vengeance and responsibility, 60–
     68
Hardy, M. J. L., 86–87
Hasluck, M., 101
Hector, 30–32, 34, 53
Helen of Troy, 24, 42
Hess, H., 100, 102, 145
Hobsbawm, E., 101–2, 107–9, 113,
   122–4, 144, 145
Hobbes, 96
Homer, 33, 34, 46
Honor. *See also* Feud; Vengeance
   demand for, 97
   mafioso, 97
   Onorata società, 97
   rituals of, 96
   vengeance, 95–98
Horbach v. State, 121
Horkheimer, M., 46–47
Horowitz, I. C., 86
Hutton, J. H., 101

I

Ianni, F. A. I., 145
Iliad, 24, 27–28, 30, 32–34, 37
Injustice. *See also* Vengeance

Iphigenia, 42
Isaacman, A., 123

J

Jachmann, G., 35
James, J., 55, 103. *See also* Bandits;
   Social bandits; Cultural traits of
   bandits
   avenger of injustice, 112–13
   legend through oral history, 113
   social bandit or culture hero, 112–
     14
   story of, 108–112
Jewish World, 163
Jones, E., 14, 22, 35, 66–68
Jones, V. C., 122
Jung, C. G., 10, 22

K

Kansas City Times, 103–18, 124
Kerényi, K., 22
Khomeini, Ayatollah, 151
King, C. B., 122
Kirk, G. S., 10, 22
Klapp, O., 162
Klockars, C., 144
Kooistra, P. G., 122–24
Koran, 69, 74–75
Kronos, 11–12

L

Laertes, 62
Latovche, R., 86
Lawrence massacre, 110
Lazzari, R., 87–88
Ledda, A., 87–88
Levin, I., 161
Lewing, L., 122
Lex Salica, 71–72
Lex talionis, 22, 52, 76
Liang, R. D., 86
Lone Avengers, 146–61. *See also*
   Vigilante
   accomplishments of, 168
   alienated, 152–55
   the ghost of vengeance, 168–69
Lone Ranger, 150–61
   third party, 151

Lorenz, K., 7
Lotterman, A., 161

M

Maas, P., 145
Mafia. *See also* Vengeance
  American Mafia, history of, 139
  balance of power, 105
  bandits, v. the, 131–32
  brokers of vengeance, 125–43
  crime as duty, 125
  development of feuding, 98
  differing functions, 131
  dispute settlement, 130–31
  familial organization, 135–36
  leadership, 128
  mafiosa way, 125–26
  manifestations of, 127–28
  Mimic of the State, 129–31
  necessity for order, 129–30
  organization, 127–29
  retribution, 137–38
  rise of Mafia materialism, 138–39
  rule of silence, 141–42
  source of conflict, 137
  use of violence, 129–30
  vengeance, 137
  vengeance to deterrence, 134–38
Mafia Method. *See also* Mafia; Vengeance
  appropriation of honor, 136–37
  deterrence, 138
  mafia retribution, 137–38
  organizational control, 135–36
  protection, 134–35
Mailer, N., 122
Malinowski, B., 102
Manzon, P., 34
Marongiu, P., 101
Marx, K., 85, 98, 99, 101
  "class consciousness," 120
  economic theory, 90, 93, 94
  exchange value, 95
  total scarcity, 90–91
McAnany, P. D., 47
Menelaus, 26, 42
Mercer, A. S., 121
Merton, R., 20
Middle East, The
  blood feud, 72–73
  "diya," 74, 75

"rajab," 73
"thar" (revenge), 73
  vengeance cultures, 76
Mills, C. W., 35
Minerva, 34
Moberly, W., 47
Mohammed, 74, 75
Montgomery, W. A. H., 87
Mosaic Law, 22
Myths. *See also* Vengeance
  creation, 11–12
  justifications of, 10
  meaning of, 13–14
  rationality, 14
  process of punishment, 20
  similarities among, 10
  superheros, 147–52
  western culture, 147

N

Newman, G., 15, 23, 52, 53, 58, 86,
  87, 101, 145, 161, 162
Newell, P. E., 122
Newsweek, 1, 8, 162
New York Times, The, 7, 8, 162

O

Oedipus, 13
Offenses
  honor, 83–84
  property, 82–83
O'Malley, P., 122–124
Ophelia, 61, 62
Orestes, 42–45, 107
  archaic forces of vengeance, 43
  trial of, 42–45
Outlaw-hero, 108. *See also* Social
  bandit

P

Pantaleone, M., 144
Paradox
  criminal as hero, 107–21
Paris, 24, 32
Patrocles, 31–32
Peleus, 25
Pelops, 42
Penelope, 36, 40, 46
People, 163

Peristiany, J. G., 87, 95, 101
Peters, E. L., 99–102
Phelps, T. G., 122
Pitre, G., 144
Pigliaru, A., 88–89
Pinkertons, 111
Pitt-Rivers, J., 101
Plummer, H., 105
Polonius, 61–62
Poseidon, 37
Priam, 24–32
Private armies, 127. See also Mafia
Punishment. See also Vengeance
    ambivalence, 70
    blood vengeance, 84–85
    classification of gravity, 54
    cultural justification, 10
    god as avenger, 74–75
    historical use of, 10
    matched to crimes, 53
    moral reflection, 53
    Mosaic tradition, 75
    mutilation, 77
    obedience, 9, 15, 18, 52, 66, 82
    obedience and moral justification, 15
    pain, 53
    proportionality, 84–85
    quality, 53
    quantity, 53
    rationality of severity, 54
    reciprocity, 9, 15, 20–21, 46, 52, 56, 66, 82
    reciprocity and moral justification, 15
    responsibility, 85
    social control, 18
    societal use of, 70
    symbolic reflection, 54
    vengeful punishment, 50
Punitive Society. See also Punishment
    origins of, 15

Q

Quantrill's guerrillas, 110

R

Racquette, The, 163
Rank, O., 147–48, 161

Reciprocity. See also Punishment; Vengeance
    animistic basis of, 18–21
    birth of social order, 56
Reich, W., 86
Retribution. See also Punishment; Vengeance
    religious, 52–53
    secular, 52–53
Rice, O. K., 122
Richardson, R. N., 121
Robin Hood. See also Social bandit
    legend of, 112
    Robin Hood Ethic, 112
Rouse, W. H. D., 34, 46

S

Sardinia. See Feud
    code of vengeance, 81–87, 93–98
    culture of violent behavior, 81
    Falchi faction, 77, 78
    mutilation as vengeance, 77
Schwartz, G., 86
Sciascia, L., 143
Settle, W., 123–24
Servadio, G., 144
Shari's law, 76
Simmel, 96
Sisphos, 37
Social bandit
    American Civil War, 109
    Antonio Silvino, 108
    ascription of social function, 114
    balance of power, 112
    Billy the Kid, 107
    cultural traits, 114–119. See also Cultural traits of the bandit
    Dick Turpin, 108
    Gary Gilmore, 107
    ideological basis, 113
    Jack H., 107
    James, J., 107, 108–21
    lone avenger, 150
    Lone Ranger, 150–161
    Mafia, 131–132
    Manolas, 108
    Nayan, 108
    Ned Kelly, 108
    press, support of, 111
    primitive rebels, 108
    Pancho Villa, 108, 113, 116, 118

Robin Hood, 108
Salvatore Giuliano, 132
Zapata, 108, 116
Social contract, 70
Social control. See also Punishment;
    Vengeance
  deterrence, 138
  feuding as, 98–99
  punishment, 138
Social order, 21, 66
  mythology, 27–29
  resultant of a feuding process, 69–
    70
Sonnichsen, W., 102, 104, 121–22
Steckmesser, K., 122–23
Stenchke, W., 122
Strachey, J., 59, 162
Superheros. See also Myths
  Batman, 148, 149
  Hercules, 147
  image, 154
  "macho," 148
  mission impossible, 148
  Moses, 147
  Nazi hunter, 155–161
  Oedipus, 147
  pursuit of vengeance, 149. See
    also Vengeance
  social bandits, 148
  Superman, 149
  Wiesenthal, S., 155–161. See also
    Wiesenthal

T

Tatum, S., 123
Texas. See also Feuding
  feuding in, 103–107
  Texan code, 103–104
Thetis, 27, 30
Thyestes, 42
  curse of, 42
Time Magazine, 1, 162
Total scarcity. See also Feud; Marx
  fear, 91–92
Transactions in homicide, 100
Thurnwald, R., 102

U

Ugolino, 48–51, 58

Ulysses, 30, 35, 47, 117
  punishment of, 36–46
  vengeance, 36–46
  vengeance to avoid death, 38
USA Today, 162

V

van den Haag, E., 7
Vasdravelles, I. K., 123
Vellacott, 43, 47
Vengeance
  absence of law, 27
  administration of, 71
  advocacy of, 4
  ambiguity of authority, 27–28
  ambivalent identification, 63
  anger, 24–34
  archaic forces of, 43
  "blood vengeance," 7, 84–85
  characteristics, 33
  civil, 42–45
  code of Islam, 74–75
  coercive nature, 50
  common bond, 27–28
  community sentiment, 4
  compensation, 74
  continuity of feuding, 99–100
  cost of, 33–34
  crime, 3–7
  cultures of, 69–85, 93–98
  cycle, 5, 159
  decomposition of the sense of in-
    justice, 29–33
  definition, 1–2
  desire for omnipotence, 166–168
  divine intervention, 28–29
  early development, 9–22
  economic factors, 80
  envy, 166
  expiation, 51–53. See also Expia-
    tion
  folk poetry, 99
  ghost of, 168–169
  giving order to, 54–55
  guilt neutralizing, 64
  homicide as "debt," 99
  instinct, 1–2, 22, 33
  instrumental factor, 137
  internalization of, 61–63, 67
  "juridicial procedure," 41
  justification, 57

legal tolerance of, 4
magic of vengeful exchange, 165–166
maintenance of order, 41, 85
manifestations of, 164
moral basis, 74
motive, 3
mutilation, 77
myths, 9–22
name of justice, 70
natural solution to conflict, 38–39
nonspecific aggression, 33
"normal defensive aggression," 2
obedience. See Punishment
"organized violence," 69
political economy of, 90–100
political factors, 80
preservation of one's life, 38–39
private character, 3
protest, 103–121
punishment, 45, 51. See also Punishment
"rakia," 99
rebellion, 167
reciprocity. See Punishment
"redemption of debt," 99–100
responsibility, 60–68
retaliation, 43
retribution, 6, 33, 42–45
right to execute, 76
rituals of honor, 96
role in history, 159
Sacred, 48–58
Sardinian code, 81–87
scale of justice, 50–51
self-protection, 2
sense of guilt, 64–65
sense of injustice, 15–18

social banditry, 167
social control, 6, 85
social protest, 120–121
symbolic transformation, 53–54
transfer of responsibility, 67
transformation into honor, 119
universal force of, 1–3
vigilantism. See Vigilante
Vengeful culture. See also Vengeance
origins of, 18–21
Vigilante (Vigilantism)
lone avengers, 146–61
principles, 104
vengeance as motive, 3, 105
vigilante committees, 104
violence, 105
Violence
Texas lawlessness, 103–104

W

Wallace-Hadrill, J. M., 86
Washington Post, The, 163
Weber, M., 35
Wiesenthal, S., 155–63. See also Superhero
avenging Prodigy, 155–6
lone avenger, 158–61
Nazi hunter, 155–61
story of, 156–8
superhero, 155–61
Wolfgang, M., 81, 87, 88, 122, 145

Z

Zeus, 12, 27, 28, 30, 32, 34